Unwrap

Eric Suddoth

RISING SMOKE PUBLISHING

Unless otherwise indicated, Scripture quotations are from:
The Holy Bible, English Standard Version ®, ©
2011 by Crossway, a publishing ministry of Good News Publishers.
Use by permission. All rights reserved worldwide.

Rising Smoke Publishing
ISBN 978-1-949869-21-7

To my family who unknowingly inspired this book during our Friday night suppers during COVID. I will always remember and cherish those drives, eating in our vehicles in the parking lot, and listening to the Christmas hymns of old.

Merry Christmas

Table of Contents

Luke 2:1-7

In those days a decree went out from Caesar Augustus that all the world should be registered. This was the first registration when Quirinius was governor of Syria. And all went to be registered, each to his own town. And Joseph also went up from Galilee, from the town of Nazareth, to Judea, to the city of David, which is called Bethlehem, because he was of the house and lineage of David, to be registered with Mary, his betrothed, who was with child. And while they were there, the time came for her to give birth. And she gave birth to her firstborn son and wrapped him in swaddling cloths and laid him in a manger, because there was no place for them in the inn.

O Little Town of Bethlehem
"the hopes and fears of all the years"

Do you know where you are from? Not just your birthplace, but where your ancestors originated? It seems like the new fad in the last few years has been administering DNA tests to find our origins.

I do not have a very common last name, at least not in the area I live. Every once in a while, after I introduce myself to someone new, they ask if I am related to so-and-so. I always reply with, "No, I don't know of any other Suddoths besides my immediate family."

A few members in our family decided years ago to dig into the ancestry a little and they came to the conclusion that we are from the England/Ireland area. That seemed reasonable since my hair has a red cast and I do not tan very well.

A few years ago I took my mother to Ireland on vacation. As we were driving around the quaint island we stopped at a place that had ancestry records. We looked up the name, and once again it was confirmed we were of Irish/Scottish decent.

I finally knew where I was from as another reliable source agreed with what my aunt had previously uncovered. Even though it was interesting to know where my ancestors were from, it really didn't change my outlook. My great-great-great-so-and-sos may have been from Ireland or Scotland, but I am from a small town in Western Kentucky.

It is interesting to know where you are from, but I think the more important aspect in life is where you are going.

You may have been born into a rough family – a black sheep of a black sheep family. When people look at you they may immediately recall tarnished memories of your older brother or sister, your drunken mother, or abusive father.

When I went to school I was constantly asked, "Do you have an older sister?" Since I was the youngest, I was always 'Lori or Amy's little brother'. Their history didn't give me any bad raps, but the teachers knew me from my sisters.

My mother also worked in the school system, so if the staff didn't know me by my sisters they would sometimes ask, "Are you Janie's son?"

I was known.

It is good to be known.

Bethlehem is a well-known town in Christianity because Jesus Christ was born there, but it was known a little before Jesus' birth. This is where David's ancestors were from and where he was anointed King. In fact, the city is often referred to as the City of David. The Jews were waiting for their Messiah to be born in Bethlehem from the word of the Prophet Micah.

But you, O Bethlehem Ephrathah,
who are too little to be among the clans of Judah,
from you shall come forth for me
    one who is to be ruler in Israel,
whose coming forth is from of old,
    from ancient days. Micah 5:2

Bethlehem wasn't a large city or widely well known, but it was still known as the birthplace of the upcoming Messiah. Bethlehem had some big shoes to fill. Sometimes instead of having a blemished family name, your name may be revered. People may have lofty expectations just because your brother was the star athlete or your sister was the valedictorian or your father was class president. It may be troublesome to have to live up to the high expectations of being just as great as those who came before you.

Bethlehem was expected to bring forth someone great. It was expected to bring forth the Savior of the world. Yet, when Jesus came into the world it wasn't with a booming announcement. The majority of Bethlehem didn't know what just happened when Jesus was born.

I love the line in this charming song:

"the hopes and fears of all the years"

It is interesting how the words 'hopes' and 'fears' are so closely linked in this song, yet they are on completely different sides of the spectrum as hope is full of light and fear is full of dark.

In this world I see a great divide in people's outlooks on life. I can talk to someone for a short period time and quickly discover if they are full of hope or full of fear. If someone is full of hope, they are positive, even in the face of adversity. They may not have a clear path, but they are optimistic of the journey. People with hope can see the dark, but instead of dwelling in the pit they are in, they look up and see a hole with the possibility of getting out.

On the other side, there are people who are living in fear. Fear of not being good enough. That fear breeds more fear and pessimism until it becomes a breeding ground for negativity. People may say they are a realist, but that is a nice way of saying a pessimist. People with fear see the dark pit they are in and won't even dare to look up and consider it is plausible to get out. Looking up just reminds them of another hurdle they have to overcome – a hurdle they don't believe they can get over.

God doesn't want us to live in fear. One of the underlying culprits of fear is worry. God definitely doesn't want us to worry. Worry is focusing solely on our problems, whereas prayer is focusing solely on God. The two are so close. We can go to God in prayer with our problems, fears, and worries, but when we give it to Him we have to give it to Him. We can't take it back.

So often when we pray to God with our fears, it is like we just want to verbalize to God how we are feeling like a counseling session, and when the time is up we pick up the fear and place it back on our shoulders and walk away. "Talk to you tomorrow, God. Same time, same place?"

But God doesn't want us to take back our fears. He wants us to leave our burdens at His feet. He wants us to relinquish the responsibility of "I can take care of it," and let him wear the crown. He wants us to surrender ourselves to him.

This Christmas season you may be battling some gigantic fears. You may think these words sound nice and pretty, but the follow through is too difficult to just toss aside the fears like balls of lint in your pocket. But to God, your fears are as miniscule as those balls of lint. If God could create a star in the heavens that's so bright you can see it from your backyard even though it's millions of light years away, then God can handle your issue. And even though God created that blazing hot star that we will never be able to see up close, it shouldn't mean we can't approach God like that star.

God is fully approachable.

There is no amount of fear where God will say, "Nope, that is too big for me to handle." There is never a wall too tall that God will say, "Wow, that obstacle is beyond me." There is never a hurt too deep that God will say, "I don't know how to fix that."

God is the God of our hopes, and He should be the God of our fears. If you can trust God to help you achieve your dreams when you're in a state of euphoria, you can trust Him to help you overcome your fears when you are in a province of depression.

God doesn't want to be God of just part of your life.

He wants to be God of all of your life.

He wants to be God of your highs and your lows.

He wants to be God of your own little town of Bethlehem that may seem insignificant to the rest of the world but is so important to Him that He would stop the entire world if you just invited Him in for a night. He doesn't care you haven't figured it out yet.

If Jesus left the glories of Heaven to be born into a stable in Bethlehem, He will gladly come and stay among the manure in your life if you will just invite Him in. But if you invite Him in, don't expect to stay in your current situation. Jesus didn't stay in the manger. He didn't stay in Bethlehem. He didn't come to Earth to stay unnoticed.

He came to change it.

Maybe it's time to make a change for you.

Are you going to focus on your hopes? Or are you going to dwell on your fears?

There is a right answer here.

The LORD is my light and my salvation;
   whom shall I fear?
The LORD is the stronghold of my life;
   of whom shall I be afraid? Psalm 27:1

But I will hope continually
   and will praise you yet more and more. Psalm 71:14

God,

Show me the reason for the hope I should have and help me to give You the fears I should not keep. Amen

Joy to the World! The Lord Is Come
"Let earth receive her King"

Do you have joy? Maybe a better question is: do you want joy? It seems like at Christmastime people are making a list of things they want: a sweater, a video game system, some new cookware. Then everyone has a list of things they want but are harder for money to buy: a trimmer waistline, a head full of hair, world peace. But does joy make your Christmas list?

Too often I hear people talk about joy as if they are speaking of happiness. They are beaming with a bright smile, boasting of God's faithfulness in His provision and answers to their prayers. But would they be smiling if God's provision wasn't what they had wished for? Would they be grinning from ear to ear if God had said no?

We tend to confuse happiness with joy and then give God praise in the happy moments.

But when was the last time you were filled with joy as you were bawling in pain? When was the last time you beamed a radiant smile as the world crashed all around you? Joy is looking to God when the sand is shifting beneath your feet and you know that even if you fall, God will be there to catch you. A smile isn't needed to show joy, but it does help.

I'm an optimist. I try to see the light in the darkest of moments. Not because I am trying to overlook the pain, but because I am trying to see through it. I'm trying to see God on the other side of the foggy mess I find myself in. I'm trying to find God in the darkest nights when the moon and stars are hidden behind a blanket of storm clouds. I'm trying to feel God even when I've grown numb to the pain. It's not that I never have down days. It's just that in those down days I try to see God more than I see my problems.

Some days I succeed and other days I fail. But God is too good to keep lingering in the failure mentality. God is too big to avoid looking to Him when I'm facing an obstacle. God is too wise to undermine His plans for my life that are meant to give me a hope and a future.

So, do you need to add joy to your Christmas wish list?

I think we all need to add a little joy to our stocking.

I sometimes hear people say in a condescending tone, "Fake it till you make it." They are saying that I fake my smile, or overlook the bleak situation, or ignore the problematic elephant in the room. And maybe I do. But I would rather be my own cheerleader encouraging me to have hope than sulk in a state of despair.

Scientists have been studying the effects of smiling for years. It has been proven that the act of smiling causes a chain reaction of releasing endorphins or happy, feel-good hormones. You may fake a smile at first, but eventually your brain will start releasing these positive sensations, and your fake smile may form into a real one.

But I'm not giving this example to oversimplify the human body and its conjunction with joy. I'm just suggesting that God, the creator of the universe and endorphins, designed us with the ability to smile in order to release these positive feelings. Feelings God whispers and sings over us all the time.

You are amazing! You are My masterpiece! You are My treasure! You are My beloved! You are the apple of My eye! You are My love! You are My child! You are My prize! You are My everything!

What if the endorphins are just another way God answers your prayers? You can count my question as absurd, but don't count out God's ability in any situation.

I'm not sure anyone can sing "Joy to the World" without smiling. The song doesn't slowly build like many songs; rather it smacks you in the face in its booming first few notes. It doesn't cater to self-reflection but is an anthem of Christ's birth. Can you imagine the composer of the melody? Can you see him behind a piano lightly playing the song as if playing "Silent Night?" The song would have a totally different feel.

No, the writers of this carol wanted to portray the exuberance of praise to the creator of Heaven and Earth. They wanted this song to proclaim with exclamation marks. They wanted this song to be an anthem of hope. A fixture of grace. A song of joy.

A line that stands out to me is early in the song is,

"Let earth receive her King!"

Did you see the exclamation mark? We are not to receive Jesus like a Christmas sweater that isn't our color. We are not to give a fake smile as if holding up an unwanted gift for a family photograph. We are not supposed to receive Christ like a spoiled brat with a hundred other presents under the tree.

We are supposed to receive our King! Receive Him with delight. Look upon Him with bewilderment. Gaze upon His grace and mercy with astonishment.

Can you recall your favorite Christmas present you received as a child?

My mother tells me of the time my grandmother bought me a little scooter and my eyes widened with excitement. She still brings it up that she wished she had given me the present because I had never ignited with so much happiness over a present before. Even as I am nearing 40 years old, my mother still remembers how I acted when I got that blue and white scooter. I still remember riding it around my neighborhood for years with my other elementary friends. It was a great present.

But no matter how good of a present you have received, have you ever received Christ with that type of awe? Have you ever poured over His words and read them as if God Himself was reading you a bedtime story? Have you been so entranced with the God of the universe that it took your breath away?

We are such a materialistic society. I, too, fall victim to wanting the flashier things in life. But it is sad when we get more excited over a scooter that will age with flattening tires and rust than we do over a personal relationship with our creator.

May you receive the true present of Christmas this season -- a gift that is purer than gold. A gift that is more precious than diamonds. A gift that will stand the test of time.

May you receive the true joy of Christmas. And may you experience a joy so uncontainable that you have to shout it out at the top of your lungs. It's okay. We are called to shout it out. Jesus said, "I tell you, if these were silent, the very stones would cry out."

Don't let God's lifeless creation give Him more praise than you.

Use your lungs to praise His name. Use your hands to clap in praise. Use your feet to stomp in praise. Use your body to dance in praise. Use every part of your body to give Him praise. And when you get tired, smile.

Make a joyful noise to the Lord, all the earth;
Break forth into joyous song and sing praises!
Psalm 98:4

A joyful heart is good medicine,
but a crushed spirit dries up the bones. Proverbs 17:22

God,
Help me to receive You like I should. Amen

O Holy Night
"and the soul felt its worth"

How much is your soul worth? That question may sound lame, but the truth is, every day we sell our soul for very little. We trade our integrity and character for a nice payday and a bump up to rub some flashy elbows. We downgrade our moral code to fit in at the neighborhood block party and the clichéd cliques that run rampant at the soccer games and housewife circles across America. We sideline our true identity for a plastic bejeweled nametag given by the Hollywood and YouTube social elite. You may not see yourself as a sellout, but we all have done it at least one time, if not more.

There may be some who would contend that their soul is worth its weight in gold – nothing. That it is a figment of a religious person's mind to make them feel better about themselves.

Then there may be some who view their soul as a priceless treasure. But how easily do treasures lose their luster and intrigue? I do believe there are some people who could stand in awe of a Van Gogh in a museum for hours. I think I could stare at *The Starry Night* for hours and be mesmerized by the swirling shades of blues and yellows.

But if I had the picture in my living room, would I stare at it for hours on end? Most likely not. The same can be said for the famous sites around the world. Do you think Roman citizens look upon the Coliseum with wonder every time they walk by it? Do you think the Parisians gasp at the splendor of the Eiffel Tower every time they see the metal tip alongside the clouds? Do you think the Chinese feel humbled as they peddle their bikes beside the Great Wall of China?

No.

Sadly, the human heart grows calloused toward the things to which we've grown accustomed. Think about your own life and the city where you live. Are there things that people travel for hours to come see or do while you look at it as if it's nothing great?

A few years ago I was showing a group of young teenagers around my hometown for an afternoon. I didn't know what to show them because I didn't think there was anything worthy of display. So, we went downtown and walked the few blocks. We came to the riverfront and they stared in awe. One of the young women looked at me and said, "I bet you come down here all the time." I smiled and shook my head no and they all were shocked. They lived in an area where rivers and lakes were not common, whereas I drove by this riverfront a few times a week. It had lost its wonder on me. But spending ten minutes with these teenagers woke my heart. They caused me to try to see the things I considered common as something more, because in all reality the riverfront is a glorious sight to see no matter the time of day or season.

God's creation is one that deserves to be marveled.

But aren't we God's creation? Aren't we something that deserves to be marveled with some awe and bewilderment? Yet, we don't. We have grown accustomed to the sparkle in our eye that our loved ones go wild about. We have grown stale to the freckles on our cheeks that we cover up with a thick layer of makeup. We have become aloof to the beauty that exudes our entire being and see only a reflection of what we saw yesterday.

It's easy to see how so many people turn to eating disorders, drug additions, self-loathing, and suicide. We cannot see ourselves as anything that deserves worth because we believe we have seen something new and exciting that is worth more than us. Yet, if you ask the person you are looking at what they see in their reflection, they will probably tell you what you tell yourself.

This song "O Holy Night" is probably my favorite Christmas carol of all time. I love the slow build of the song as if it is constructing a firm foundation. I love how the melody is soothing and comforting in the first few lines. Then the pace of the song picks up and I cannot help but sway to the music. Then the dramatic chorus hits me as if I'm not expecting it even though I have heard it so many times before.

I love the chorus so much – the reverent plea to adore the One who has created all things. The song begs us to not hold anything physically back in our worship. It calls us to fall before the one that will also stand strong. It is beckoning us to remember that glorious night of our Savior's birth. It is in that chilling moment when God put on flesh and left the comfort of Heaven to come and live a life not worthy to be known or remembered.

There is so much to love about this song, but the line I love the most is,

"Til He appeared and the soul felt its worth"

Some may wonder why this line resonates so much with me. Out of the entire song with its beautiful poetic lines, why does this simple line that many overlook make me want to stop and stare at it?

I think it goes back to the line before it: "Long lay the world in sin and error pining." This is such a depressing line, and I think many people don't want to dwell on these words. But the truth is, the world is not a good place. It is a place of death, decay, violence, suffering, pain, and hate. If we had a welcome sign for visitors I could see it reading something like, "Earth – Look Past Our Mess."

Yet, despite our flaws; despite our shortcomings; despite the bad decisions and cruel mistakes; despite the corruption we point out and the starting points in our own lives we try to hide; despite the ugly truths and the sadistic lies; despite the Brutus' backstabs and the Judas' kisses. Despite everything we showcase, God still loves us.

He sees past the lives we live. He sees past the lives we try to show. He sees the truth and still loves us.

Jesus' entry into this world is an interesting take on God's salvation story. God created the world perfect, yet people had to go and mess it up. Then he gave them rules to follow, yet people had to go and mess it up. Years passed and people still had to go and mess it up. Jesus came to fix the broken cycle so nothing would separate us from God anymore. Our sin still tries to mess it up, but Christ's blood redeems us.

Imagine the world before Christ. If you wanted to be close to God, it was a never ending cycle of do good – mess up – perform a sacrifice – reconciliation – do good – mess up – perform a sacrifice –

reconciliation – do good, and so forth. No matter how well we try to live, we mess up daily.

Yet God loved us so much He sent His son, Jesus, to perform the ultimate sacrifice – His own life, becoming the ultimate reconciliation. Even though we still mess up daily, we don't have to become separated from God through our faith in Jesus Christ. We do lose the intimacy when sin messes things up, but it can be quickly recovered.

Before Christ, the soul was worth the price of a sacrifice of an animal or good given in exchange with repentance. That bird or crop may have been sacrificed, but most likely there would be another animal or crop to take its place. It wasn't a sacrifice the sinner had to endure. The sinner had to watch something else take its punishment for the wrong he did. It may have been humbling to watch a lamb die for his sin, but it might not have brought full remorse for his soul.

And then came Jesus. A perfect man who lived a blameless life. A man who loved the loveless. Who befriended the outcasts. Who spoke words of life to those the world ignored. He encompassed all that was good. And He died for all the crummy, despicable, shameless, tasteless things I do. He died a death I deserve to die every day for the acts of treason I do to God's holy face. He died the death so I wouldn't have to.

So how much is your soul worth?

It's worth dying for.

They say people on their deathbed hardly ever ask about their finances, or their real estate property, or their stock portfolio. They don't ask for someone to bring them their priceless heirloom to touch as they pass away. They don't mention for someone to bring them their last bank statement. You can put a value on a lot of things in this world, but some things are valueless.

Your soul is beyond value.

Your life is priceless.

God wants you to see your worth because He saw it the moment He created you. If He didn't think you were worth anything, He wouldn't have wasted His time on you. Yet, He knows the number of hairs on your head. He knows what you think about all the time. He knows your doubts and your fears. He knows your regrets and your failures. He knows more about you than you know about yourself. Yet, despite everything, you tell yourself no one will love you.

He loves you.

He has always loved you.

And He will always love you.

So, why do I love this little line from this beautiful song? Because it reminds me that when the chips are down, when COVID is rising, when I'm pressed against the wall, when I don't see a silver lining, when all I see is a bottle of pills or blade as a way out – He sees so much more.

He sees us as worthy. He sees us as loving. He sees us as good. He sees us as His child. He sees us as someone who might have wandered but is now home. He sees us as the best parts of ourselves, even when we can't see them at all.

I think that is the best news, and we need to share it more often.

He restores my soul.

He leads me in paths of righteousness for his name's sake. Psalm 23:3

For what does it profit a man to gain the whole world and forfeit his soul? Mark 8:36

God,

Thank you for seeing me as worthy of such a love as yours.

Amen

What Child is This?

"The Virgin sings her lullaby"

Have you ever truly wondered what made Jesus so special? We read the Bible, we see the miracles He performed, and the amazing acts of love and grace He displayed, but so often we decompartmentalize the God incarnate with the baby Jesus. But they were the same person. Little six-second-old baby Jesus was the same one who died on the cross for our sins.

I know when I read the Bible so often I read the scriptures for the religious meanings and context, but the book is also a book of history. I've often heard people refer to 'Bible characters', and when I hear that I instantly think of books that are fictional. When you read a biography, do you call the people in the book 'characters'? When you watch a documentary or reality television show, do you call the people 'characters'? Most of the time I hear people call them by their names, but I rarely hear someone say, "Those characters on 'Duck Dynasty' are hilarious." They usually say, "Uncle Si is hilarious."

You may be wondering what I am getting at, but we have to realize Jesus wasn't a fictional character who fed the five thousand, walked on the seas, healed the sick, loved the loveless – He was a real man just as Winston Churchill, Jimmy Stewart, Christopher Columbus, and Elvis Presley.

When I teach my group of young men, I try to convey to them that Paul wrote the book of Philippians while he was under house arrest or in prison. He was a real man writing a letter to another real group of people in a real church in the real city of Philippi. Adding that groundwork to the Bible adds another dimension. It is like when you get a Christmas card from your Aunt Charlene in Boise. She is a real woman who took time out of her day to write a card to you. There is a personal touch from getting something as personal as a letter. In some traditional Christmas cards the writer gives a yearly synopsis of the family. That is what the entire Bible is – a love letter synopsis of God's workings. The next time you read the Bible, look at the personal touches. Anywhere you read you should be able to see them.

So my question remains: what made Jesus so special? I think the better question may be, what makes Jesus so special?

I always find the missing sections of the Bible the most interesting. What happened between Jesus' birth and when he was a small boy going to the temple? How was his life as a teenager? What did his friends think of him in his twenties? The gaps we will never know, but I am sure He lived life like the rest of us with one significant difference. He lived it sinlessly.

I believe he experienced the highs and lows that also shadow over us. Did he perform any miracles when he was a child? Who truly knows, because it is stated that the first miracle He performed by turning the water into wine was the first of his ministry in Cana. Did he perform miracles for his family beforehand not to bring glory to the Father? I find these mysterious gaps fascinating, but those gaps do not hinder my faith; it's just intriguing.

Christmas time is an exceptional season to wonder and ponder. There are so many things that are unknown, so let your mind drift. We have the foundation of Mary and Joseph in a stable in Bethlehem and a few other added insights, but the rest is a wonderful mystery.

One of the mysteries is what Mary was feeling during that night. We can read in Luke 1 what Mary was thinking months before giving birth. But we never read what she was feeling the night of Jesus' birth.

A beautiful Christmas hymn "What Child is This?" is a stunning telling of Christ's birth; then a section fast forwards to His death and then circles back to his birth. When I hear this song, I can picture a movie of the life of Jesus with sporadic flashbacks to that meek scene in Bethlehem.

There are multiple beautiful lines in this carol, but one that stands out to me is,

"The virgin sings her lullaby"

This line shows the intimacy Mary must have been having with her newborn son just as most mothers would be having their first night. I can picture her scared teenage eyes looking into Jesus' and diving head first in love with her son at that first glimpse, letting all her fears dissolve into his soothing gaze. I can see her smiling and rubbing his little cheeks, counting his little fingers, feeling the stubble of his finger nails. I can imagine her leaning down and kissing the top of his head. I can close my eyes and see her inhaling that baby smell and smiling at the aroma.

But most of all, I can see her singing a song to her baby boy as she holds him tightly wrapped in her arms. She could have sung him a traditional Jewish lullaby, or maybe it was a song her mother sung to her as a young girl, or maybe it wasn't a song with words, but a soft wordless hum of exceeding joy mere words could not express.

Whatever she was doing, I can imagine she was recalling all the moments that led her to holding her newborn son. The moment when the angel Gabriel came to her and said she would be with child. The moment when she felt the spirit of God rain down on her. The sideways glances she received in the marketplace as an unwed mother starting to show a little belly. The worrisome look on her parents' faces as they sent her to her aunt and uncle's home. The hard conversation of telling her future husband she was pregnant. The overwhelming relief when Joseph agreed to wed her. The tiresome journey to Bethlehem as she was on the verge of labor. The terrifying moment her contractions started and the women of her family were miles away. The moment of relief when she heard the first stifled cry of Jesus.

I've seen on television shows and movies the first moments mothers have with their newborns, and it seems there is an instantaneous connection. Mothers immediately start to envision what their newborn will grow up to be, dreaming lofty fantasies of unbelievable proportions. But to a mother, anything is possible for her baby.

I wonder what Mary was dreaming about for Jesus. She had been welcomed by an angel telling her she was going to bring forth the Messiah that generations of her family had been waiting for. I could see her looking down at her little baby boy and thinking of those same big, lofty dreams of him changing the world.

Thirty-three years later she witnessed Him changing the world through His death on the cross. I do not think that is what she was smiling about in that Bethlehem stable. No good mother ever wants to see her child suffer.

Sadly, the dreams and aspirations mothers have the first night with their newborns rarely come to pass.

But it is still lovely to dream of the rich life your child will have. Jesus had a full life, reaching the potential He was destined for. It just wasn't the way Mary had envisioned.

You may not have reached the potential your mother had for you, but your life isn't over. The God who opened seas for men to walk can open doors for your next step. The creator who causes sunflowers to move with the sun can cause all the obstacles to fall out of your way. The savior of the world who defeated death with a mere breath can defeat your biggest enemies.

You may think you haven't reached your potential, but none of us have. We are all striving to reach what God had destined for each one of us. So if you are struggling, take heart, because you are not alone. If you feel you are at the end of your rope, hold tight, or not – maybe fall into the hand of God who has been holding you since the moment He dreamed of you.

Don't give up on yourself because there are many people who haven't given up on you yet. You may not have had a mother who dreamed lofty dreams for you the day you were born, but God's dreams for you are much, much better than someone's earthly ones. You may not have had a good relationship with your mother, but God loves you more than you could ever know. You may have bitterness and hate for the woman who gave you up, but God never gave you up. He's still watching over you like a proud dad. Even when you mess up,

He's still there taking snapshots of everything you do, framing them for everyone to see.

When God made you, He stopped what He was doing and took the time to count out every one of your hairs. He looked at the stars and wanted your eyes to twinkle just the same. He found a beautiful shade of sand and wanted your hair to shimmer the same way. You may see just a reflection of a person with a hard life, but God sees His masterpiece.

And I'm pretty sure God was humming when He made you because He was thinking of some incredible dreams for you to achieve.

And I'm pretty sure He's still humming over you – waiting for you to see the limitless future that lies ahead.

The LORD your God is in your midst,
a mighty one who will save;
He will rejoice over you with gladness;
He will quiet you by His love;
He will exult over you with loud singing.
Zephaniah 3:17

And God saw everything that He had made, and behold, it was very good. And there was evening and there was morning, the sixth day. Genesis 1:31

God,

Open my ears and my heart to hear you singing Your lullaby over me. Amen

The Little Drummer Boy
"Then He smiled at me"

There is something wonderful about the gift of music. Science has studied the benefits and discovered it helps the listener's mood, lowers stress and provides comfort, helps us sleep better, improves memory, reduces depression, and many other benefits. That is why music is used in many types of therapies today. There is some supernatural power in music.

I have seen videos of patients suffering from dementia, and when they hear a song they know, they instantly light up. Something in the music takes them to a place before they were ill. They immediately feel the passion they had once. It is like the music awakens them to the person they used to be. I don't understand how the brain works, but I wonder if that is why the Bible constantly tells us to praise God through musical means. Maybe He knows a little bit about our inner workings since He created them.

The book of Psalms in the Bible is one of my favorite books. Psalms is a collection of lyrics written by various authors (David; Asaph, the son of Korah; Heman; Solomon; Moses; and Ethan, the Ezrahite). This book contains the worship songs of the Jews thousands of years ago. Also, many songs we sing today are derived from verses in this poetic book.

Songs were not just mentioned in Psalms; throughout the Bible people praise God through songs. They are praising God for the miracles He performed, their protection, their provision, their joys, and their triumphs. But they were also singing to God in their moments of sadness, during the deaths of loved ones, when God seemed distant, and when they were in need of a miracle. Music doesn't discriminate. There are songs to be sung with a smile on your face and there are songs to be sung with tears. But in either song, God desires us to sing to Him.

When I was in the sixth grade I joined my school band. I played the trumpet. Well, I use the term played very loosely. My sisters would tell me I sounded like a cow dying, so I didn't stick with it. Later I found out my band teacher praised my playing, but it was too late. I had already decided to quit. Years later when I was in high school, a few of my friends played the guitar. I didn't want to be like everyone else so I started toying around on the piano, learning chords. I still cannot play very well, but I love to sit behind my piano and play. It is a place I can go and worship God one-on-one. I seldom play in front of anyone, so it is like my own private sanctuary. It is a moment where everything is left behind and I can come with only my heart and klutzy fingers.

I think that is why I love the song "Little Drummer Boy" so much. The whole song revolves around the idea of this poor little boy having nothing to his name, yet still coming before the baby Jesus to give him all he has – his song.

A line that stands out to me that gives me chills when I sing it is,

"Then He smiled at me"

I believe that little line evokes the heart of God in the simplest of terms. I often wonder, "Do I make Him smile?"

What do you think makes God smile?

Do you think He smiles when He looks at you?

I don't think He sits up in Heaven and smiles at everything we do. We mess up. We make mistakes. I believe we sadden God when we do not do as we should. Those moments when I follow my own heart and not God's are moments I not only cause God to grieve, but also myself. I would love to say my songs to God are mostly songs of praise in joyous times, but if I am truly honest, I would say the majority of my songs are in thankfulness for the mercy He bestows on a wayward child. The mercy and grace He doesn't have to give, yet gives in abundance without any strings attached or conniving contracts for my soul.

Yes, that is why I sing. Because I have so many reasons to try to make Him smile at me. I may sing off key and I may not play the right note, but I hope He can see my pure motives. I hope He can hear beyond the melody of my voice and hear the cries of my heart. I hope in those moments I cause Him to smile a little more than He was before.

Some may say praising God is trying to earn salvation, and the only way to receive salvation is through faith in Jesus Christ. I totally agree with the part that one can only receive salvation through faith in Jesus Christ. But if you have been totally changed, if you have become a new creation, if you have realized that you were technically dead before Christ came into your life, wouldn't you want to sing? Wouldn't you have something to sing about? Nothing I can ever do will earn me salvation. I could feed the poor every day of my life, but if I do it to gain something, I am doing it for the wrong motives.

God sees through our motives. Nowhere in the Bible does it say that a good person will enter the Kingdom of Heaven. But hopefully, a sinner who has found Christ will try to live a better life to cause his savior to smile.

Wanting God to smile isn't a rouse to get Him tied around your finger in order to get what you want like a spoiled child. No, wanting God to smile is a response for our thankfulness for treating us like His children when He didn't have to take us into His arms and show us His love – the love He displayed on Calvary through His painful death.

So, the question goes out once again – Do you make God smile?

I think if you take a moment and reflect on that little question, He will smile a little more. When you come to God with just your heart and tell Him how you feel about Him, I believe He smiles. And if you bring along a little drum, I bet He taps His feet to the beat as well.

For you will not delight in sacrifice, or I would give it;
you will not be pleased with a burnt offering.
The sacrifices of God are a broken spirit;
a broken and contrite heart, O God, you will not despise.
Psalm 51:16-17

And to love him with all the heart and with all the understanding and with the strength, and to love one's neighbor as oneself, is much more than all whole burnt offerings and sacrifices. Mark 12:33

God,

Show me what makes You smile, and I hope at times it is me.

Amen

Sweet Little Jesus Boy

"Our eyes were blind, we could not see"

When you see an image of the baby Jesus, what do you see? Do you see a sweet little baby boy, or do you see the image of God? I think that is why people celebrate Christmas so much more than they celebrate Easter, because it is easier to look at a newborn baby than a dying man.

I have never wanted a child of my own, but I have heard from many people about the longing to have a child. I have heard women yearn for the pitter-pattering of feet down the halls. I have heard men talk of wanting a little one to teach how to fish or play baseball. There is something remarkable about having a child to call your own. To raise the child with the best characteristics of yourself and hope they rise a little taller than you have risen yourself.

Easter should be the holiday Christians celebrate louder, because that is the day Christ was resurrected from the dead proving to the world once and for all He was who He said He was. Easter is the remembrance that He opened the tomb along with every tomb that had been sealed before Him and every tomb that would come after Him.

We celebrate Easter with pastel eggs, furry rabbits, cute outfits, and baskets filled with candy and treats. But the celebration is nothing compared to the spectacle of Christmas. One holiday remembers an agonizing death of a grown man and the other commemorates the birth of a little baby boy.

It is easier to smile and sing Christmas carols of a savior who came into the world than it is to sing crucifixion songs of death and sin. Both are important in the grand scheme of our faith because we couldn't have Easter without Christmas. But we wouldn't have Christmas unless there was an Easter – that is where the difference lies.

I know it is human tendency to read the Christmas story in the Bible and picture a quaint family being thrown into an unfamiliar situation, ignoring the fact that in thirty-three years that family would go through a horrific loss. We like the shiny lights on a Christmas tree that symbolize the light of the world, but we don't like to look inside ourselves and see the light of the world had to come because of the darkness in us all. We don't like to admit that if we hadn't messed up, the little baby born in the city of David could have lived a long, happy life. But the truth is, our errors, our flub-ups, and our self-centeredness were the reasons that little baby boy didn't live a long, happy life.

We can play the blame game that Adam and Eve caused the fall of the world, but if you were Adam or Eve, I bet you would have fallen as well. I know I would have. The Bible doesn't say how long they were in the Garden of Eden. It could have been years before they were tempted. Or it could have been thirteen minutes and seventeen seconds. We might try to point a finger at the generations who walked on Earth before Jesus was born and say Jesus suffered because of them.

But he also suffered because of our generation. Christ died not just for the people who had wandered away from God three thousand years ago, but for people who are wandering today and in the years to come.

A little Christmas carol that I do not hear very often, "Sweet Little Jesus Boy," has a haunting line:

"Our eyes were blind, we could not see"

There are a few stories in the Bible of Jesus healing the blind. They had been blind their entire lives and suddenly they were able to see. I cannot imagine living in that type of darkness and suddenly being able to see what I was only able to feel and touch a few minutes earlier. The blind person was able to see the faces of their friends and family. They didn't have to use their imagination anymore, but they could actually see.

I don't think the writer of this song was speaking of physical blindness. I think the writer was speaking to us who put up blinders so we don't have to see the messy parts of the world. We put up blinders to not get involved in the human trafficking situation that affects millions of innocent children. We close our eyes to overlook the pleas of strangers for help as we lock our car doors. We ignore the world because the world doesn't fit into our neat little Christmas box with shiny blue wrapping paper and a glossy white bow.

If we notice all the people who are living and possibly suffering today, that may put us in an uncomfortable situation; we definitely put up blinders when we celebrate the Christmas season. We sing the carols, watch the movies, smile at the sugar cookies waiting for Santa, but we overlook the true picture of Christmas of God's sacrificial lamb being held by his earthly mother.

If we took the little baby Jesus from Mary's arms and sacrificed Him like a lamb on the alter, crowds would be in an uproar. Yet, when

He died in front of His mother's trembling empty arms thirty-three years later, we speak of His crucifixion with clichéd church rhetoric.

That little baby boy had the weight of the world on His shoulders from the moment He took his first breath. If He didn't do everything He was supposed to do, everything would fall apart. God's plan would have crumbled, and Satan's hopes would have exploded like a celebratory firework.

That little baby was just a little boy with a hard life ahead of Him. A harder life than anyone else would ever live. It is said that He experienced every type of temptation and overcame it. I do not know if he experienced every type of pain, but I'm fairly certain that as He was dying on the cross He felt all the pain we have ever felt. All the pain people are bombarded with through sexual abuse, schoolyard bullying, backhanded smacks from guardians, emotional wounds caused by hateful words from trusted people. He may not have walked in your shoes, but He felt your pain, and He felt it so much that it caused Him to die.

You may not see the little baby boy in the manger as someone who came to Earth to save you, but that is why He came. Because you are not strong enough, smart enough, good enough, brave enough to save yourself. You may think you are, but you aren't. You need someone to be your hero. You need a Superman figure who can do the impossible. You need someone who will forever be on your side. You need someone to have your back when you feel alone. You need that light when you are wandering in the darkness. You need that source of hope when you are pressed into a corner. You need that rescuer to come in and save the day, to carry you out of your burning life before it crashes down on you.

And He did.

You may not see Him as a hero when He's wrapped in swaddling cloth. But not all heroes wear a cape.

He exchanged his crown of gold for a crown of thorns. He replaced his bracelets with a pair of nails. He turned in his slippers for bare, splintered feet. He gave up his flowing robe to die naked. He gave up the applause of angels to hear the chants of haters.

That sweet little Jesus boy doesn't deserve for us to overlook Him with the image we want to see. He deserves the utmost honor. He deserves complete devotion. He deserves for us to remember the reason He came down to Earth.

He deserves for us to open our eyes and see the truth.

Master you have shown us how

Even when you were dying

Just seems like we can't do right

Look how we treated you

But please sir forgive us Lord

We didn't know it was you

Sweet little holy child

We didn't know who you were

Blessed are the pure in heart, for they shall see God. Matthew 5:8

And the Word became flesh and dwelt among us, and we have seen his glory, glory as of the only Son from the Father, full of grace and truth. John 1:14

God,

Help me to see. Amen

Away in a Manger
"And stay by my side"

Every time I see a nativity scene, whether it's on people's front lawns, Christmas cards, or on display at my mother's house, I cannot look past the manger. It was just a feeding trough. It was a lowly crib of hay sitting in the middle of a stable with cows and sheep. It was the bare minimum.

I wonder what Jesus thought of the plan. He had to leave the perfection of Heaven where everything was at His fingertips. He left the streets of gold for a bed of golden hay. He left the crystal seas for painful crystal tears. He left the pearly gates for the impurity of the world. He left Heaven to come down to us – people who needed saving.

I have rarely gone anywhere I didn't want to go. Usually the places I don't want to go are because they are not comfortable or familiar. They are typically with people I do not know or are different than me. It is the feeling of uncertainty I do not like. I do not like change or the feeling of having to bend without reasonable cause.

If I look more closely, I guess it is out of selfishness. I do not want to feel uncomfortable because it is giving a little too much of myself to try something new. And giving too much of myself is hard when I don't want to do it. Isn't that what selfishness is in the root? Self-centeredness is when you focus all your attention, all your cares, all your feelings, all your worries on yourself and no one else.

We are a selfish world.

No matter how we try to spin it, most of our life is grounded in our own selfishness. Yes, we can do things that are good, but we seldom do things that are good without giving ourselves a proverbial pat on the back. On the 90's sitcom "Friends", there was an episode when Phoebe was trying to prove Chandler wrong by doing good things without getting any pleasure. She spent the entire episode searching for that elusive good deed, and if my memory is correct, she never found it. No matter what she did, she felt something.

We are emotional, feeling beings. We let our feelings direct our paths. We let our emotions guide our steps. We let our consciences point us in the way we need to go. And since it is our feelings and emotions, they usually lead us to places we want to go.

There are some people through history that have lived lives that I would say were not self-centered. We hear stories of self-sacrifice or martyrdom for a cause, and my mind cannot fathom such a devotion to lose one's life for someone else.

I recently went to France and rented a car and drove to the beaches of Normandy. I spent an afternoon walking along one of the beaches where thousands of men died to protect the freedom I have. I walked over the sand leaving footprints, but those brave men left a much more lasting impression. My footprints disappeared once the tide rose with the moon, but I hope their impression will be remembered for many years to come. As I stood on the beach I couldn't help but feel remorse for the lives that were lost. But also remorse in myself because I'm not sure I could have done what those brave men accomplished as they swam upon the beach knowing they would likely not live to see the end of the day.

I often wondered if the soldiers knew what they were getting themselves into as they were heading to France from their base in England. In Normandy there is a museum dedicated to the Ally invasion. I walked through the quiet halls and looked at the articles of history. I looked at the photographs of soldiers that died a few miles away on that cold beach. Then I watched a film in the museum about the invasion. I was shocked to hear stories from soldiers who survived and how they knew what they were getting themselves into. That as they were loading in their boats in England the priests were giving them their last rites because they knew they might not return.

And yet they still went to fight.

Those brave men might have fought for many different reasons. They might have been thinking of their loved ones back home, keeping the Nazi regime from heading toward America. They could have been thinking of themselves as little boys who always wanted to fight and go to war. They could have been thinking of themselves and their desire to live another day. No matter their reasons for going, they still went and fought.

I do not deserve the sacrifice they made for my sake. But as they were fighting, they were not thinking of me. They didn't even know me. A few might have known some of my family members, but the majority had never heard of the Suddoth name. I was not on their mind when they were fighting, but that doesn't diminish the respect I give them.

I go back to wondering how Jesus felt when God said He was going to be leaving the freedom of Heaven to go into a stormy occupied land of hate and hostility. Jesus may not have landed on the beaches of Normandy, but his thirty-three years of life were leading him to His own beach of Normandy called the hill of Calvary.

So often as we sing this Christmas carol we picture a defenseless little boy surrounded by his mother and father in a stable with loud, rowdy critters. Yet, Jesus wasn't as fragile as we picture him to be. He may have been a baby boy wrapped in swaddling clothes, weighing six pounds and five ounces, but He had the power of Heaven coursing through His being. He was the one who was with God the Father who created the celestial stars overhead. The star that led the wise men was a star that was created by Him.

He left His lavish estate to be a son of a lowly carpenter.

It is the classic rags to riches story in reverse. We hear the horrors of bad investment mistakes causing millionaires to become penniless beggars. Christ went from being the richest to the poorest in a blink of an eye.

I love this Christmas carol for its simplicity. I can see Mary rocking her little baby boy, kissing His forehead, singing Him a tender lullaby while hushing the baby lamb nearby. Dads may not be able to multitask, but mothers can always do three things at once.

A line that stands out in this song to me is,

"And stay by my side"

It's a simple line, five little words, five little syllables, but it packs a punch.

Jesus came to Earth not because we were perfect and we deserved Him. He came to Earth because we needed Him. He came because we were not perfect. He was our soldier coming to protect us because we needed protecting.

Not very many people would come and protect those who didn't deserve to be protected. But Christ came, even while we were still sinners.

And He did not just come, do his job, and leave. No, He stays by our side.

He stays by our side when we are wallowing in the pits of sadness and despair. He stays by our side when we are trying to put the syringe down. He stays by our side after we have cursed our loved ones to their faces. He stays by our side after we do all the unmentionable things we do each day, and still He never leaves us. He stays by our side even after we deny His existence.

He doesn't do so because we deserve Him.

No, He stays because He knows we don't. He sees beyond the mess we find ourselves in. He sees beyond the rubble of our own self-destruction. He sees beyond the fiasco of self-hate. He sees beyond the lowly state we are in and stays by our side.

Maybe that is why He was placed in a manger.

Because no matter how low we are in this world, He will always come to be by our side. He was laid in a manger on His first night on Earth; He isn't too proud to come and spend night in your dark alley. He isn't too proud to come and spend a night in your lousy apartment. He isn't too proud to come and spend a night in your broken-down car.

No matter where you are in this world, He will stay by your side til morning is nigh.

And then til night is morning.

And then again til morning is nigh.

He won't just stay by your side for one night, but for every night you ask Him to come.

And knowing him, He will be by your side even when you don't ask.

Because He didn't come because we asked Him; He came because He knew we needed him.

Do not be afraid of them,

for I am with you to deliver you,

declares the Lord. Jeremiah 1:8

And behold, I am with you always, to the end of the age. Matthew 28:20b

God,

Please stay with me now and forever. Amen

Luke 2:8-20

And in the same region there were shepherds out in the field, keeping watch over their flock by night. And an angel of the Lord appeared to them, and the glory of the Lord shone around them, and they were filled with great fear. And the angel said to them, "Fear not, for behold, I bring you good news of great joy that will be for all the people. For unto you is born this day in the city of David a Savior, who is Christ the Lord. And this will be a sign for you: you will find a baby wrapped in swaddling cloths and lying in a manger." And suddenly there was with the angel a multitude of the heavenly host praising God and saying,

"Glory to God in the highest,

and on earth peace among those with whom he is pleased!"

When the angels went away from them into heaven, the shepherds said to one another, "Let us go over to Bethlehem and see this thing that has happened, which the Lord has made known to us." And they went with haste and found Mary and Joseph, and the baby lying in a manger. And when they saw it, they made known the saying that had been told them concerning this child. And all who heard it wondered at what the shepherds told them. But Mary treasured up all these things, pondering them in her heart. And the shepherds returned, glorifying and praising God for all they had heard and seen, as it had been told them.

Angels We Have Heard on High

"Which inspire your heavenly song?"

Have you ever heard a songwriter tell the story behind their songs? I love going to concerts and hearing the reasoning for the songs that I connect with. To hear from the artist's heart where they were in the moment they scribbled the lyrics. To imagine the first time they plucked the strings on their guitar or let their fingers dance on the ivories to come up with the contagious melody. It is inspiring to hear how they take a little line or a few notes and form a song that people will be singing even after the writers have died. Every song has a story.

Every life has a story as well. It can be a constant belly-laughing comedy. It can be laced with fragile heart-wrenching tragedies. No matter how your life has been or is going to be, it is a story that was written before the dawn of time. Your life may not be as you wished, and most likely, it's not the way that God had dreamed as well.

God envisioned a life without sin for each one of us, and that mucky sin is what causes the problems we see in our world and in our lives. Without sin, the world would be a constant paradise. But even though God had one perfect life planned for your existence, He also knew that perfect life wasn't going to happen. That is such a strange thought that God had a plan for you but knew you wouldn't stick to that plan. So, often I hear people say, "Well, if God knew that was going to happen, why did He let it happen?"

That is where our finite minds cannot grapple with the infinite mind of God. I had someone explain it to me that in our mind, time is on a line, each second building upon one another. So what happened ten minutes ago ultimately impacted what we are doing now. But God is beyond time. I have heard some people theorize that God jumps around in time. He isn't bound to a constraint as we are; He can go to June 28, 1304 and also go to June 29, 2029. It's an interesting concept to understand how God knows everything and allows everything, yet He still had a good and perfect plan for each of our lives. It's just a theory, but it's one my finite mind can partially understand.

You may think your life isn't anything special. No reason to write an autobiography or memoir. No one would care to read about your troublesome youth, no one would sit still long enough to flip through the pages of your twenty-something years, and only a few would browse through the pages if they had nothing better to do.

Yet, God would read through the little 400 page book that barely scratches the surface of your lifetime and beg for more. He would point out to you the moments you should have put into your book, because He already knows everything about you. He knows it all and still loves you.

I don't know how anyone can go through the Christmas season and not have a warm hot chocolate moment thinking about angels. We use angels as decorations, scattering them through the limbs as ornaments and possibly placing one on the top of the tree. We light up large plastic angels on our front lawns and plaster them on greeting cards with lovely sayings of "Peace" and "Good will toward men" with a glittery glow.

Angels should be highly regarded, not just at Christmas time, but throughout the year.

Interestingly, we tend to picture angels singing in the movies, Christmas pageants, on greeting cards and even in Christmas carols, but nowhere in the Bible does it say angels sing. Some people infer that angels sing because it says the angels praised God, but praising God doesn't necessarily mean singing. There are verses that mention singing, but they don't specifically reference angels singing.

Could angels sing? Quite possibly. I'm not counting anything out in the realm of God's possibilities. Anything is always possible when God is in the middle of it.

So, the song "Angels We Have Heard on High" may or may not actually be true. We are not sure. Someone has pointed out that just because the Bible states the angels were "saying", doesn't mean they couldn't be singing because singing is a type of saying. But a line that hits the songwriter's love of mine is,

"Which inspire your heavenly song?"

The song may be asking the angels or shepherds this question, but I think it is a question we should all ask ourselves.

You may say I am not a songwriter. I don't know how to play an instrument. I don't know the first thing of poetry. I don't know how to write a song.

But in a way, we all know how to write a song. How many times have you hummed a melody you created on your own when you were thinking or cooking or working? We all do it. All throughout history people have sung while they worked, even the seven dwarfs. So, to say you can't write a song isn't human. I don't know how many times I've hummed a tune without thinking.

Love makes you do silly things sometimes. Watch any musical and you will see men sporadically singing their raw feelings and emotions to the love of their life. The Hollywood magic of Gene Kelly, Bing Crosby, Christopher Plummer, and Hugh Jackman are examples where the men came to the realization they were in love and had to sing.

There is something humbling and authentic about singing to your love. And what person doesn't get a little emotional when someone is singing a song directly to them? And then to add a layer that the person wrote this song as they were thinking about you -- that is the magic of songwriting. Because it isn't just a song being sung, it's the formation of the entire song from start to finish with that one person in mind.

So, what are some things that inspire you to sing? Is it the love of your life? I know parents sing spontaneous lullabies for their children as they are rocking them to sleep. It is a tender moment of hugging your child in your arms and knowing that you would do anything for them to keep them happy, even singing the words from your loving heart.

I wonder if God wishes we would sing to Him like we do to our earthly loves?

When we sing to God, so often we sing like it's a military command. The music has started at church and it is my key to sing the words projected on the screen or in the hymnal. But how often do we sing a song to God for no other reason than to sing Him a love song?

Have you ever sung to God a love song for His ears only? This Christmas season, why not give that a try? Turn off the television. Sit in silence. Bask in the twinkling lights from your tree. Let the thought of a loving God sweep you away to a place you have never been before.

Then hum Him a song.

He doesn't care about the words if it's coming from your heart.

And then as time goes on, maybe words will come. But if they don't, don't worry. I believe He will take great joy in the sound of your heavenly song.

Oh sing to the LORD a new song;
sing to the LORD, all the earth! Psalm 96:1

Oh sing to the LORD a new song,
for he has done marvelous things!
His right hand and his holy arm
have worked salvation for him. Psalm 98:1

God,

Hum hum hum hum hum hum hum. Amen

Angels, from the Realms of Glory
"Mercy calls you; break your chains"

Do you ever think about where the angels are? Where is this realm of glory we sing of? I truly believe there are angels in Heaven praising God, but I also believe there are angels among us. A verse that I love is,

Do not neglect to show hospitality to strangers, for thereby some have entertained angels unawares. Hebrews 13:2

Have you ever entertained angels? What if we all have entertained angels and were unaware of their presence? We assumed they were a stranger on the street, but what if they were a messenger from God? We pass by people every day without acknowledging them, but who is to say they are not angels? Who is to say that a realm of glory isn't here on Earth? Christ came from Heaven to bring Heaven down to us, so what if angels are a part of our daily occurrence and we are just unaware?

I like to think about angels watching over me. I like to close my eyes when I am falling asleep and believe that an angel is standing guard making sure nothing will get me while I sleep. It may be a childish wish, but if there are angels there has to be something on the other side of the spectrum. Just as there is light, there has to be darkness.

I do not like to think about the other former angels that God created with a divine purpose but fell away. That part of the story shakes me to the core to know if there is an angel watching me sleep, there is probably also something else watching me. The only comfort I find in this is knowing God has always won.

Yes, there is a battle going on that we cannot see. But God is bigger than the other side. God is all powerful, so nothing can defeat Him. God is all knowing, so nothing can surprise Him. God will overcome like He always has.

So often at Christmas we like to only see the angels with their white flowing gowns flying with their beautiful wings and golden halos. We don't like to think of the other side, but the truth is we have to stay alert, or we can be easily swayed to thinking that the other side isn't real. I have heard it said many times that the greatest deception of Satan is convincing the world he doesn't exist. It is interesting because most powerful people love to boast and take credit for their successes. But Satan isn't like most people. He's not looking for a temporary success; he's trying to make an eternal lasting mark.

I don't want to dwell on this topic too much, but it is something to remember. If you do not stand for anything, you will fall for anything. Do not fall to his deception that he isn't real. Don't fall into the deception that God isn't real either.

Some people find freedom in denouncing religion and charting their own course, but by turning away from God's freedom in grace, you are actually binding yourself to chains of disbelief. Do not deceive yourself by believing the notion of who you believe God to be. That god you have concocted is a false god. God doesn't need you to tell Him who He is. He already knows who He is. He just wants you to know the true Him.

But I hear so many people say, "Well, I think God is like …" and their only reason is because that is how they want God to be. When we start to tell God who He is, we have put a fake god on a pedestal and sealed the real God in a box that we will never discover.

In the Christmas carol "Angels, from the Realms of Glory," there is a lovely line that surprised me:

"Mercy calls you; break your chains"

We are all tied down by some type of chain. Some chains are visible for anyone to see in the form of reliance on drugs and alcohol. We see the proof of people's chains in their verbal and physical attacks of hatred for another human. We find the links of the heavy chains weighing them down with their depression and anxiety. Then there are chains that people hide like a golden necklace. They hide their insecurities and self-loathing while looking in the mirror as they get ready for work. They push the chains of personal addictions under their beds beside magazines and videos. They polish their chains of envy or pride like it's a precious heirloom.

We all have chains. But God came to break the chains. To break the bondage that causes us to lose sleep at night with fear and worry. To shatter the shackles we confuse for comforting when they are really squeezing us numb. To take away the knots that hold us down causing us to never see our full potential.

Christ came to Earth not to point out our chains with condemnation. He came to help us get out of them. That is the difference between Heaven on Earth and Hell on Earth.

Hell wants to inflict the pain. Hell wants us to believe we deserve the chains. Hell wants us to succumb to the fact there isn't any use in believing in something better. Hell wants us to forget the words of Christ that echo with love and mercy. Hell wants us to turn away from God and sink deeper into the pit of rusty chains without any keys. Hell wants us to lose hope.

But Christ is all about hope. Christ was the one who told the woman at the well to come and drink of the water that would never dry. Christ was the one who befriended the sinners and went to their houses for supper and companionship. Christ was the one who stopped a customary death and pointed out that the woman sinned just like everyone holding a stone.

Some may feel guilt when they speak of God, but that isn't the God we celebrate at Christmas. That is the god they formed in their own minds.

Christ is all about giving mercy to those who need it. Christ doesn't ever leave a chain unbroken. He never looks upon a sinner and thinks, "You deserve that burden." He never smiles at the pain the shameful suffer at their erroneous ways. He never scoffs at our pleas for mercy.

He listens to our unrighteous prayers with attentive ears. He stops what He is doing and hangs on every one of our words as if it's a Shakespearean sonnet. He doesn't point out the miswordings or phrases. He doesn't correct the grammar or add a comma or period in one of our run-on rambling rants. He listens to our prayers and smiles.

So often we think our prayers are all about our words, but I love the first three words of that line: Mercy calls you.

You may think you are reaching out to God, but He is actually the one doing the reaching. You may believe your words are causing God to break the chains with your touching prayers, but God's mercy is what broke the chains long before you asked Him.

I wonder, are we chained by our sins? Or are we sitting in the rubble of our broken chains thinking we are still chained up?

I have seen some people training their dogs on leashes, pulling them back when they get too far away. After many times of getting pulled back, the dogs realize they are not allowed to go that far ahead of their human. A well-trained dog can go for a walk and never get pulled back on its leash because it knows the limit. I have even seen their humans drop the leash to show that the dog will not go too far ahead because the dog knows not to.

The leash was used as a training tool to help the dog know its bounds and to keep it safe, but the dog didn't realize the leash didn't hold any power anymore.

So often I believe God has mercifully broken the chains that hold us back, but we are not merciful to ourselves to see His hammer of grace. We cannot forgive ourselves for the mistakes of our past. We can give compassion to others, but we cannot give it to ourselves.

If you have turned to Christ, you have no chains. He has already broken all the chains holding you down. You are His beloved! Wouldn't a loving husband do anything for his wife? Wouldn't he do anything to make sure she was loved and taken care of? So why do you think God hasn't taken care of you?

Stand up and walk away from the rubble of your chains and find mercy in the hands of Christ who has already destroyed every chain that you could ever imagine. If you feel shackled, it's not because God hasn't undone them. It's because you haven't.

Embrace your freedom by embracing Him.

Therefore, since we are surrounded by so great a cloud of witnesses, let us also lay aside every weight and sin which clings so closely, and let us run with endurance the race that is set before us. Hebrews 12:1

For God did not send his Son into the world to condemn the world, but in order that the world might be saved through him. John 3:17

God,

Thank you for mercifully breaking all my chains. Amen

Hark! The Herald Angels Sing
"Pleased as man with men to dwell"

What pleases you? What are some things that bring delight to your heart? What are some things that warm your insides? What causes you to smile like a five-year-old on Christmas morning?

I love to travel. Whenever I uncover an affordable plane ticket to take me to some new, unfamiliar place, my heart skips a beat. I get those butterflies in my stomach as I start to plan my trip, and I research everything I can to make sure my trip goes smoothly. People may think I don't have a fear of flying since I book flights often, but I still get those nervous knuckles, saying a quick prayer with my eyes closed as the plane takes off. Then when we land my anxiety doesn't settle, but it kicks up a notch because now I am where I have been dreaming about for the last month. I breathe very little between the airport and my hotel, but once I get to my hotel and can put up my bags, then my heart is fully pleased.

I don't like to get lost in Zurich as I'm pulling my luggage behind me looking for my hotel, but I am fine getting lost in the history of the city two hours later with only a light jacket and backpack. Because once I find the hotel, I at least know where to go to get back to my home away from home.

I tend to not travel to the same place twice, but when I do, it is usually because I am traveling with someone who hasn't been there before. A few years ago I traveled to Europe with my sister and niece, and we explored London, Paris, and Ireland. It was a great trip. I tried to get my mom to go with us, but she passed. Then when she saw the pictures of Ireland, she wanted to go. So, the following spring I took her to Ireland and drove on the left-side of the road around the island with all their roundabouts because I wanted her to see the places I had already seen.

Would I return to Ireland on my own? I'm not sure, even though there are so many other places still to see in that lovely island. But there are also so many other places to see in Iceland, a place where I have never been. But if someone wanted to go back to a place I had been, I would definitely take them, because it pleases me to share in my love of traveling.

Have you ever truly considered what pleases God?

I feel like we all have the church-approved answers of praying, reading the Bible, going to church, worshipping Him on Sundays. But do you think those answers really please Him? Do you think we can fit God into a box of Top Ten Answers for how to please Him?

Do you think you please God?

You may think those two questions are the same, but they aren't. We may believe we know what pleases God, but do we actually do it? Or do we pretend to be the perfect Christian on Sunday and then live like the devil through the week?

I have to admit that for years I didn't realize there was an exclamation mark after hark in the Christmas carol "Hark! The Herald Angels Sing". I thought it was a poetic line or maybe Hark was a name of a group of angels. But Hark means to listen. It is commanding us to stop and listen to what the angels are saying. It is not something we are supposed to take lightly. We are not supposed to multitask by making our grocery list as we hear the Christmas story. We are supposed to stop and listen.

How often have you stopped and listened this Christmas season? I mean truly stopped what you were doing and listened to the heart of the Father.

If you are still wondering what pleases God, I think that would be one of them.

A line from this boisterous song that causes much deep thought is,

"Pleased as man with men to dwell"

Do you believe God is pleased with you? And is He pleased with you so much that He would leave Heaven to live among you as your next-door neighbor, as your schoolyard chum, as your peaceful co-worker?

I sometimes wonder if I was alive during the time of Christ coming to Bethlehem, would He look at me and think, "Nah, Eric's not worthy of me dwelling beside him."

If I look past the twenty-four hours and I weighed my good deeds against my bad, which would be heavier? Would God look upon the scales and be pleased? Would He be pleased enough to come dwell beside me now?

I hope I please Him. I hope when He looks upon me I bring a smile to His face just as I smiled when I took my mom to Italy and showed her the beauty of the Venice Canals. I hope I bring delight to Him with my walk of faith as I found delight getting lost in Quebec City with my parents when we were touring Eastern Canada. I hope

He doesn't get tired of me like I don't get tired of my travel mates during the week of trains, planes, and automobiles.

But if I'm honest with myself, would I be pleased with myself from the outside looking in? If I rewound the day and replayed every sideways glance I gave in haste, every snicker at someone else's expense, every cruel thought and envious stare, would I be pleased with my actions for the day?

That is what surprises me so much about the love and grace of God the Father. He sees all that I do. He knows all that I think. He hears all that I say and don't say. He witnesses the moments I fail in solitude and the moments I boast in social circles. He doesn't just see my polished Facebook posts and witty tweets, but He sees the deleted moments I don't ever want to rehash. He hears the unflattering words I wish I could take back. He knows more than anyone else, including myself.

Yet He still chose to dwell with us.

He could have lived a life in plush estate, keeping the riff-raff away, yet He beckoned the untouchables for a merciful embrace. He laughed with the deaf as their hearing was regained. He grinned with the blind as their vision was sparked. He leapt with the crippled as their legs sprung into action.

He could have remained sitting tall on a lofty throne, yet He bent down. He bent down to be among us because He knew we would never be able to climb up to His throne on our own. We needed His help.

Yet, so often as He bends down now, we push aside His outstretched hand. We ignore His smiles as we close our eyes. We cover our ears so we don't have to hear His compassionate voice. We fall to the schemes of our own devices because we don't think we need His help. We chastise Him like He's an annoying kid brother. We ask Him to stay out of our way and to go back home. And when He wouldn't listen to us, we nailed Him to a cross to try to keep Him in His place.

He died for the sin in our hearts. The sin He saw long before we knew of a thing called sin.

He took on my blame and died a blameless death. He wore my shame and died a shameful death. He picked up my cross and bore it for my cause. He died my death because He didn't want me to die it.

He lingered in agony. He suffered in heart-wrenching defeat. He clung onto a hope for a hopeless group of people. And then He breathed His last; the world went dark; the teacher was buried; the messiah was gone; the hope of the world was laid to rest.

The story could have ended there. If He was any other person, it would have.

But He decided to dwell with us once again. Even though the world shouted "crucify", He returned for those that nailed Him to the cross. Even though the world backstabbed Him, He returned for those that held their bloody knives. Even though the world scoffed His name, He returned for those who spit in His face.

Why did He choose to dwell among us?

Because He is a better God than we would have been. That is why He is our God. Not because we are better people, but because He makes us better.

And the wonderful story of Christmas is that He still dwells among us. Even though He rose up to Heaven two thousand years ago, He still is among us through the Holy Spirit. Even though He could have left us to make it on our own, He left the greatest Christmas present to help us on our journey.

So is He pleased with us?

I still don't know that answer.

But I'm pleased He gives us a chance to please Him as He dwells among us today and forevermore.

So that Christ may dwell in your hearts through faith – that you, being rooted and grounded in love. Ephesians 3:17

And the Word became flesh and dwelt among us, and we have seen his glory, glory as of the only Son from the Father, full of grace and truth. John 1:14

God,

Thank you for seeing beyond my mess and dwelling with me anyway. Amen

Do You Hear What I Hear?
"Do you know what I know?"

What do you really know? We all have our favorite topics, guilty pleasures, and secret addictions where we know all the stats of Pete Sampras, all the varieties of cardinals, or all the subway stations in New York City.

We all have something we find fascinating. I love the Olympics. It is hard to catch me watching sports on television any other time of the year, but when the Olympics are on, I am glued to the television. But it is not just watching the Olympics that I enjoy. It's the history of it. It's the moments when a normal human being is skyrocketed to all-star status for a brief moment in time. It's those emotional highs when twenty years of dedication of early morning practices pay off, and their national anthem is played. It's hearing the back story of the athletes and the financial toll their love for their sport has cost them.

But not everyone wins at the Olympics. Thousands of athletes will compete for one chance of glory, but only a few will take home a medal.

When the fourth-place finisher leaves the track, how does she feel? When the sixth-place diver gets out of the pool, what is he thinking? When the last person in the marathon crosses the finish line, what is going through his heart?

I hope they don't see their life as a waste. I hope they don't walk away from the Olympics wondering if that's it. I hope they consider the fact that even though they didn't place, they are still better than billions of other individuals in this world. But do they know that when they leave the Olympics without that elusive medal?

Do they know they are still in a class above most people?

I would think many Olympians go to the games knowing they are not going to medal. They have that hope the impossible could happen and they could excel above the rest, but deep down, the world already has their favorites they believe are going to win.

I wonder how they feel knowing that the odds are against them.

I hope these athletes have encouraging coaches, loving families, and close-knit friends who whisper into their ears, "You are amazing no matter what happens today."

But is that really how it goes?

Or do they hear their coaches demand perfection? Or does their family stick beside them for the hopeful payout in the future? Are their friends only close for the Facebook status of saying their friend is an Olympian?

I wonder what these Olympians hear. I hope they hear the roaring crowd and smile. I hope they hear hundreds of different languages and grin at how different we are while still the same. I hope they joyfully tear up hearing an anthem being played in their event, even if it isn't theirs, with good sportsmanship of a once-in-a-lifetime moment. I hope they hear the sound of laughter and feel the pats on their back from the community of other Olympians.

I hope.

When I was a kid I wanted to attend the Olympics. Every year when the Olympics come on, I see a dream I didn't fulfill. But I believe God knew better than allowing me to be the best American in a certain sport. I'm not sure I would be able to handle the pressure. And even if no one was pressuring me, I would pressure myself to be better than the best. Yes, God knew what He was doing when he didn't graft my legs with exceptional abilities.

The song "Do You Hear What I Hear?" has always baffled me with its strange lyrics. We sing the song like nature is speaking to other living objects. We compare the grandeur of a star to a flimsy kite. We say the song is high above the trees and as big as a sea. Every time I hear this song my mind focuses on the imagery the lyricist is describing, and to me it just doesn't fit.

But in the midst of the lines that don't make sense to me there is a line that rings true to me on so many levels:

"Do you know what I know?"

And if someone asks me this during the song, I could honestly answer, "No. I don't understand the phrasing of this song. I don't at all."

But I think that is also the beauty of this song. It is about someone telling someone else who doesn't know something what they know. So, I may not have chosen the words or phrases the writer did, but I can sit beside the writer and nod my head in agreement of the purpose.

I may not know what the writer knows, but I am humble enough to listen to the story.

Sometimes in life we are the one that knows and needs to share what we know. Then there are other times we are the one that needs to listen to what someone else knows.

I'm not sure which is harder.

Is it harder to claim you know something and have the burden to share it with others or claim you are clueless and need help understanding?

If you know and believe the story of Christ, are you being like the little shepherd boy in the song and telling others? Or are you assuming the world already knows and keeping your knowledge to yourself?

I often find myself on that side of the tracks. I tell myself we live in the United States where churches are sometimes on every other corner with a big white cross on the top of the steeple. I tell myself that everyone knows that a church building is a place where people go to worship God. I tell myself that even if I don't tell them, people have listened to Christmas music, watched the Charlie Brown Christmas special, or received nativity Christmas cards. They have to know even if I don't say anything to them.

But do they really know? Do they really know what I know to be true? Or do they know bits and pieces of the gospel story that has been commercialized such that they miss the fact there is a difference between believing in God and believing wholeheartedly with complete love and trust in God?

As I sit and listen to the song, I can picture myself as the little shepherd boy watching the king from a distance assuming he must know about Jesus, because for goodness sakes he's the king of this land. And if I, a poor little shepherd boy, know the truth about Jesus, then he definitely must know.

But as I place myself in this song I can see a king who doesn't know because society has told him to achieve the American dream. I can see little kids on a playground not being taught of a God who loves them because their parents don't believe. I can see the hurt looking for a place of refuge and finding it not from the church but a dealer in a dark alley.

I was fortunate to be raised in a family that taught me about Jesus. Sadly, not everyone is as fortunate as I was.

So, do you know what I know?

The only way you would know is if someone else told you.

If everything we learn has to be told to us, why do we not tell it to others?

Why do we assume they know when assumptions often lead to misunderstanding?

Let's not make the same mistakes repeatedly. Let's share what we know with others. They may know it. They may not. The best gift you can give to someone is the gift of knowing Jesus.

I hope you know what I know.

And I hope you have enough confidence and boldness to share what you know.

I hope I can follow my own advice.

Do you not know? Do you not hear?
Has it not been told you from the beginning? Isaiah 40:21

What do you know that we do not know?
What do you understand that is not clear to us? Job 15:9

God,

Help me to share what I know about You to others. Amen

Silent Night, Holy Night
"Shepherds quake at the sight!"

What does it mean to quake? I think when we hear this word we instantly think of an earthquake – the destructive power of the Earth when the plates shift causing damage and casualties. To be honest, when I hear the word quake it doesn't give me a good feeling. It gives me a feeling of fear.

I do not consider myself to have many fears. I may be quiet, but speaking in front of loud crowds does not cause me to rattle in my bones. I have had friends who were afraid of balloons or clowns or being locked in a confined place. We all have fears. I dislike snakes. I don't know if I would call it a fear, but I think the best type of snake is a dead one. I know they serve a purpose, but when I go to the zoo and see the reptile exhibit, I just keep walking.

Fear is an interesting tidbit in our human psyche. Things that I am fearful of may not be the same as you. You may balk at the idea that I close my eyes and walk straight ahead so I do not see a slithering creature in a glass box, but I may look in confusion when you say you have a fear of tomatoes. Psychologists can study their entire lifetimes on fears and never scratch the surface of everything that fears entail. We all have a fear of something. I may not understand your fear and you may not understand mine, but that doesn't mean it doesn't exist in our own minds.

Many times when I hear the song "Silent Night" I inwardly smile to myself. Can you picture a silent night when Christ was born? Can you picture a silent night when any baby is born? Eventually the baby will settle down and the mother can finally rest in some silence, but was the night Jesus was born really silent?

Jesus was born in the town of Bethlehem during the time that Caesar Augustus issued a decree that a census be taken. People were traveling all over to return to the place of their families to be accounted for. When Joseph and Mary came to Bethlehem, all the inns were full. The Bible doesn't say, but I would assume that Joseph had other family coming to Bethlehem during this time. I would assume that most families would let someone stay the night if they had room. But Joseph and Mary didn't have a spot anywhere. The entire town was full.

Envision your hometown if it was completely full. Restaurants would be running over. Stores and markets might have their shelves bare. People might be walking the streets in the evenings taking in the sights.

Were they doing this in Bethlehem?

Or was everyone just staying at their resting place during this time?

I envision the entire town being loud.

Then we get to where Joseph and Mary were staying – in the stable or cave-like setting with animals around. I know most animals follow the sun as their schedule, but I'm pretty sure it wasn't silent. No matter the animal, they make sounds whether they are awake or asleep. And then throw a newborn baby into the mix. I can visualize Jesus crying to be fed; crying because he was tired; crying to be held; crying because the cow just lowed and woke him up. Then let's not forget the angels or the shepherds who came to witness this miracle. Shepherds most likely didn't have an accountant persona. They had a hard lifestyle of tending their sheep. They had to protect their livelihood against attacks. A shepherd was a low man on the status totem pole, and they knew it. And usually, when people have that chip on their shoulder, they sometimes tend to personalize the stereotypes. So, could the shepherd be a well-mannered individual, quiet and reserved? Most definitely they could. But could they also be a hard-skinned group of individuals that fight and don't back down to anything? That is also a possibility.

We can try to paint this picturesque image of a silent night, but I would think this was probably the least silent night. We sing this song many times in churches with candles and even a cappella to showcase the stillness.

But I think this song should not point us to the stillness of Christ's birth years ago, but to a stillness we can have today. That despite the chaos of the world, we can rest in the peace that God is in control. That even though the peace seems unreachable, we should still reach for it. It's not the image of baby Jesus sitting in a food trough that gives me peace, it's the image of my Lord and Savior reaching out His hand and saying, "Be still."

Even though I chuckle at the idea of the song, I understand the meaning behind it. I love it when we sing it at church and the music is soft and the voices are low. It brings a peace to a sometimes uncertain world.

A line that stands out to me the most of this lovely song is,

I mentioned earlier that everyone has a fear of something. It is something that causes you to quake.

But how often do you quake at the sight of God?

There are probably some people who legitimately have a fear of God that causes them to tremble in fear of Him as if He were a spider spinning a nasty web. We shouldn't have that type of fear of God. He doesn't want us to have a fear of Him that causes us to distance ourselves from His love and grace. He doesn't want us to be paralyzed in a state of fear where we wish He didn't exist. He doesn't want us to look at Him with eyes that wonder what He will do to us.

Yes, the shepherds were probably deathly afraid when they saw the host of angels. Throughout the Bible, any time an angel is introduced, it usually says, "Do not be afraid." Why is that?

Because if something just appeared to me out of the blue, I would be afraid too. Also, there are different types of angels. Some of the angels' descriptions are not the handsome men holding a harp and strumming. Angels have different levels and abilities. We do not know which type of angels appeared to the shepherds. It could have been ones that look like us, or it could have been ones that have six wings and are covered with eyes or multiple faces. These creatures God created to be messengers or protectors are not ones we should overlook.

Once the initial fear subsided, probably the second type of fear the shepherds had was a holy reverence. This is the type of fear we should always have when we look upon God.

God deserves a holy reverence from all of creation for an unlimited number of reasons. Anything God has done, He deserves to be revered for it. Without Him, none of this would have come to be.

But how does it make you feel to know that without God, nothing would have come to be? Does it make you feel less of a person? Does it cause you to realize how meaningless and insignificant you are in the grand scheme of things? Does it wake your instincts that it's not all about you after all?

I think many people quake before God when they come face-to-face with the reality that God is greater than them.

Can you stand before someone greater than you and not feel the need to humble yourself to them? Many times out of gut instincts we try to better ourselves when a co-worker gets a promotion we thought we deserved. Or when another person gets rewarded and we become envious. In those instances we may not humble ourselves to someone that is presumed to be greater. But are they actually greater? Just because someone claims someone is greater doesn't actually mean they are. There are many ways to grade someone, and they could be greater in one area and you could be greater in another.

But God…God is greater in all areas. That is the difference.

We can try to say we are smarter than God, but we aren't. We can try to say we are more creative than God, but we aren't. We can try to say all these meaningless excuses of why we are better than God, but in the end, we aren't.

But God doesn't treat us like we are beneath Him, even though He could. He could use us as pawns or dress us up like His toys, but

He doesn't. He doesn't use His greatness against us. He actually uses it to better us.

There are many moments in life I have fallen to pieces. But in all of those moments, God was there to pick me back up. Even though my messes were beneath Him, He still came and helped me. Even though He could have ignored my pleas, He never did. And He never will.

He knows everything we do. And yet, He still loves us.

I think I tremble more at that statement than anything else. To know that Christ died for me, a worthless sinner, causes my heart to hurt at the pain and suffering He endured for my sake – for my worthless, useless, penniless sake. But He didn't just die for me -- He also died for your worthless, useless, penniless sake. You may think you are worth something to your friends and family, but your worth is dust compared to the treasures God beholds. You may think that you can be used for some great cause, but God doesn't need to use you for anything.

God doesn't need us, yet He wants us.

When Christ was born and the angels went to the shepherds to tell the glorious good news, did God need the shepherds to know? Were the shepherds so important in the story that if they weren't told then everything would crumble? Were the shepherds told because they were worthy to be told?

No.

Just as God told the little shepherds that may have been an outcast in society, He is always willing to tell you the same good news of Jesus' birth. It doesn't matter what you have done in your past, He still wants you. No ifs, ands, or buts. He wants you.

If that doesn't make you shiver in your bones, I don't know what will.

Worship the Lord in this splendor of holiness;
tremble before him, all the earth! Psalm 96:9

Tremble, O earth, at the presence of the Lord,
at the presence of the God of Jacob. Psalm 114:7

God,

Help me see that You are bigger than all my fears. Amen

Joyful, Joyful, We Adore Thee
"Let Your light upon us shine"

There is something very refreshing and nourishing with getting sunlight. Science has proven that getting sunlight helps in the production of vitamin D in your body which supports bone health, lowers blood pressure, reduces inflammation, and helps with depression and many other factors that affect your immunity.

Light is a very good thing. During the dark winter months I know a few people who buy lamps to put in their homes and offices to combat the dreary gray days. There are also some friends who partake in tanning beds during these cold months to feel the warmth of the bulbs on their skin. They say it brings a sense of relaxation and gives their attitude a nice boost.

I have to admit that a couple of years ago I purchased a "happy lamp" as my friends called it. I knew some people who were experiencing the effects of seasonal depression and I recommended the lamps. As I was researching the cost I realized it wasn't very much and decided to get one for myself. My friends tend to laugh at me and my online shopping habits in the late evenings when I can't sleep. If there is a study with some scientific findings that may help with back issues, knee inflammation, or allergies, I will buy it. Sometimes these purchases end up in a box under my dresser when they don't work as the reviews stated, but sometimes I pass on my findings to my friends and family.

Isn't that what friends and family should do? When you find something that changes your life you want to share it with those you love. Friends don't keep secrets when they find the secret for joy, right?

How often do you share a recipe on Facebook? Or share a tip you learned on TikTok that blew your mind, like your car window will not automatically go up to the top if it senses something is in its way? Or share some money saving advice you stumbled upon while scurrying through Amazon's Prime Day sales?

We are a society that loves to share what we know. We share jokes around the water cooler. We share political viewpoints around the office. We share football game highlights on the assembly line. We share a recent facts or news stories at a dinner party. We share our children's proud achievements like they found the cure for cancer. We love to share.

Yet we don't share our faith as much as we should. It is like we follow the unwritten rule to not talk about income and religion with others. We have all heard the horrid stories of when someone said something about faith and it caused a breakdown in that relationship.

I know I have been there. I have hidden behind my faith that I displayed outwardly, but when friends needed to hear the truth of grace and love that only Christ could give, I kept my mouth shut. I would nod my head and console myself by saying, "They know what I believe and if they were interested they would ask."

But very rarely do people ask. Very rarely do other people take the initiative to start up a conversation they foresee to be uncomfortable. Very rarely do other people find what they are looking for in the dark.

They need some light.

They need to be shone some light.

The poem turned hymn, "Joyful Joyful We Adore Thee" is one that causes me to smile. Many Christmas hymns are lyrically solemn and somber, but this one starts off with an anthem of praise from the very beginning. I don't know how someone cannot feel the uplifting spirit while singing this hymn or reading the words. It is one that invokes praise from start to finish.

It radiates light and joy.

One of the lines that stands out to me in this lovely hymn is,

"Let Your light upon us shine"

All throughout scripture, light is mentioned as a positive reference. With light the darkness must flee, light causes fear to leave, light uncovers and exposes, and light is good.

But when we read about light in the Bible, most often it doesn't mean the light from the sun, but the light from the Son. I could shine a flashlight on you and point out the stain on your shirt from a clumsy salsa episode. But His light can point out a much deeper stain on your soul that needs to be cleansed.

That is the beauty of His light. He doesn't shine His light like a police spotlight to cause you to plead guilty and be sentenced to a life of prison. He shines His light for you to repent and be set free from the prison you are in now.

That is the surprising story of grace that sounds too good to be true. His light may expose a deadly wound, but it is able to heal and mend any gash to your heart. He doesn't stand pointing at the infection of your heart and shake His head with a surgeon's mask on saying it doesn't look good. He stands with arms spread wide to take away the guilt you have been hiding. He doesn't shake His head in disgust, but nods His head with love and compassion. He doesn't broadcast your flaws and errors with cover story theatrics, but erases the blemishes like they were never there.

The light the world shines is nothing compared to the light He shines. We live in a world where scandals are front-page news and a lucrative story for any magazine. The investigators and writers dig deep into the trenches to pull out the dirtiest, ugliest, juiciest details without regard for the damage it may cause, as long as their story gets a nice page and their name is in bold underneath.

But He already knows of all your scandals. And He hasn't told anyone.

We see so many people fall from grace in tabloids when the skeletons in their closets get exposed. One-time ideal athlete loses his golden ticket endorsements, one-time Hollywood "it girl" loses her reputation and blockbuster status, one-time songstress loses her credibility and likeability with her fans.

In one swift moment, life could crash when an unflattering light in shone on you. You may think you are not important enough to have such a wreckage displayed for the world to see. But you could still sink in your small town if a false light is shone on you. It is easier for people to spread an untrue rumor than to hear the truth. The newspapers are famous for giving an eye-catching headline on the front page only for it to be retracted a few days later hidden on page ten.

But the beauty of His light is He is never wrong. He never spreads false rumors. He never spreads true rumors. He spreads love. He spreads forgiveness. He spreads grace. He spreads hope. He spreads joy.

When He shines His light upon us, it is a beautiful experience. It isn't harmful like the rays from the tanning bed. It doesn't damage or cause sunburns or skin cancer later in life. No medical professionals will tell you to limit your exposure to His light. His light gives so much more than vitamin D. It gives the unlimited bounty of all that is good.

If you need some love, let His light upon you shine.

If you need some peace, let His light upon you shine.

If you need some encouragement, let His light upon you shine.

If you need some rest, let His light upon you shine.

May you ask Him to let His light upon you shine. And may you ask Him again and again, because you can never get too much of His light.

So, if you are struggling, ask Him for His light.

If you are hurting, ask Him for His light.

If you are in a dark place, ask Him for His light.

May you see His light – a light that will forever change what you see.

Lift up the light of your face upon us, O Lord. Psalm 4:6b

The light shines in the darkness, and the darkness has not overcome it. John 1:5

God,

Let Your light shine upon me. Amen

Hail, Thou Long-Expected Jesus
"Joy of every waiting heart"

Do you like to wait?

I don't think anyone likes to wait, whether it's at a traffic light, grocery store, or doctor's office. Waiting is aggravating. But there is usually an underlying reason for the aggravation. Are you aggravated with the shoppers in front of you causing the lagging time, or are you aggravated you have somewhere else you need to be in a few minutes? Are you really disturbed by the red light or the traffic congestion, or are you late for dinner? Are you really annoyed that the nurse is taking her time to take your vitals, or are you afraid of the outcome?

We all wait throughout the day, and it doesn't cause such an aggravation all the time. We wait in the morning for the coffee, but the wait might not seem horrible because we are doing other things. We wait when we get to work as our computer boots up, but that wait allows time to interact with co-workers and catch up on their previous night's activities. We wait as we bake a birthday cake, but that wait allows us to pick up the kitchen or even watch our latest television episode.

We do not always dread the wait when it isn't urgent.

But when we need something immediately, that is when it seems like the world has turned its back on us. When we're waiting for a phone call, all the worst case scenarios get played in our heads. When we're down to our last few dollars, pay day seems like an eternity away. When we're hurting, it seems like the healing will never come.

I think we have grown into a society of impatient people, but we have also evolved into self-centered maniacs. When we lift ourselves up above the situation going on with the car in front of us, we have entered into a dangerous zone of only thinking of ourselves. That selfish thinking can linger and trigger more disgruntled thoughts where we believe our situation is more important than anyone else's.

It is not always the waiting game that tears us apart. It is the fact that we believe everything should align perfectly for us without any problems or hindrances. But when problems do arise, the littlest things such as waiting seem to put us all on edge.

Do you remember as a kid waiting for Christmas? Do you remember counting down the days until the 24th of December? As a child it seemed like Christmas would never get here. The waiting was agonizing.

But do you remember how you felt on Christmas morning as a child? That burst of energy allowed you to spring out of bed at 5 a.m. when on any other day you would have rolled over and put the pillow over your head. That spring in your step. That excitement in your voice. That joy in your heart.

I remember.

I find this line in the Christmas hymn "Hail, Thou Long-Expected Jesus" tugging at my heart:

"Joy of every waiting heart"

It seems like an oxymoron. Who would connect the words joy with waiting? Very few.

But we need joy in the waiting. We need Jesus during those times when life is on hold. We need Jesus during those cold winter nights when the world itself seems cold and distant. We need Jesus during those disheartening seasons when hope seems like a fairy tale and tomorrow already feels like a tragedy.

Faith in Christ shouldn't give us a bleak future. It shouldn't cause us to see every cloud in the sky as a possible storm brewing its fury. Faith in Christ should allow us to have the perspective to see the dismal clouds but also have the hope of a rainbow to come.

There is a story in Luke 2 when the newborn Jesus was presented at the temple. It tells of a prophetess, Anna, who never left the temple but worshipped day and night. It is said that when Jesus was presented, she immediately started giving thanks for what was to come.

We often hear stories or teachings of this devout woman and how she knew there was something different about Jesus. But we don't know why she worshipped in the temple day and night. Was she pleading with God with a troubled heart, or was she waiting with joy?

You can sit in the temple day and night with a sulking attitude. I know many people whose prayers are fraught with worry and pain, and when they say "Amen," nothing changes. They limp away with the same worry and pain. But when we come to God we should give Him all the fears we are holding. We should give Him all the emotional pain that has rotted us to the core. We should give Him all the stress that weighs us down until we can't stand up straight.

But so often, we confuse prayers with a nagging session. God doesn't want to listen to us nag and complain without giving Him the chance to speak. When you pray, what is your focus? If your primary focus is yourself, you are missing the point of prayer.

God should be what you fixate your eyes on during your prayers. Not yourself. If you are fixating on you and only you, are you really speaking to God? Or are you just talking to yourself?

When we focus on God, all of our problems may not vanish, but it causes them to shrink in the presence of the Almighty God. When we want to see God, all the other images swirling around in our mind will fade until He is in the spotlight. When we search for Him, we will find Him.

Is it fun to search for a needle in a haystack? No. But when you find that needle, you know it. You can feel it. It may cause a little pain, but you know your search wasn't for nothing. You may have a bleeding finger, but you have some undeniable proof that you found the needle.

One of my favorite stories in the Bible is Genesis 32 when Jacob wrestled with God. When the wrestling was over, God didn't bless Jacob with perfect health or give him all of his desires for not giving up. God touched his hip and Jacob walked with a limp. You may wonder why I like this story. I love the image that God gave Jacob some tangible proof of their encounter, even if it was a limp that would stay with him until he died. Every time he took a step, Jacob would be reminded of the night when God was with him. And maybe that reminder of God being with him then gave him the joy that God would be with him when he wrestled internally.

If I were Jacob I would prefer to have something more pleasant than a limp, but I hope I could look past the pain and see the beauty in the moment.

I hope we all can look past the pains we are suffering and find the joy. It isn't easy to find the joy in the pain. It takes a lot of faith and commitment to see the joy in the waiting. But I hope you take heart that you are not alone. We are all waiting for something.

We may not always share what we are expecting, but we are all in a period of waiting. We may handle this period differently, but we can all find some common ground in looking for joy.

May we find the joy and hold onto it as we wait. You can hold onto fear, hate, and worry, but all of those things will just cause you to fester more. May we look to God during our waiting who can take away the weight we place on ourselves. May we see the God who has always been there waiting. Funny isn't it? He has been waiting for you to come to Him much longer than you have been waiting for whatever it is you desire.

Take joy in the truth that He is waiting for you.

Being strengthened with all power, according to his glorious might, for all endurance and patience with joy. Colossians 1:11

May the God of hope fill you with all joy and peace in believing, so that by the power of the Holy Spirit you may abound in hope. Romans 15:13

God,

Please come be my joy. Amen

Matthew 2:1-12

Now after Jesus was born in Bethlehem of Judea in the days of Herod the king, behold, wise men from the east came to Jerusalem, saying, "Where is he who has been born king of the Jews? For we saw his star when it rose and have come to worship him." When Herod the king heard this, he was troubled, and all Jerusalem with him; and assembling all the chief priests and scribes of the people, he inquired of them where the Christ was to be born. They told him, "In Bethlehem of Judea, for so it is written by the prophet:

"'And you, O Bethlehem, in the land of Judah,
    are by no means least among the rulers of Judah;
for from you shall come a ruler
    who will shepherd my people Israel.'"

Then Herod summoned the wise men secretly and ascertained from them what time the star had appeared. And he sent them to Bethlehem, saying, "Go and search diligently for the child, and when you have found him, bring me word, that I too may come and worship him." After listening to the king, they went on their way. And behold, the star that they had seen when it rose went before them until it came to rest over the place where the child was. When they saw the star, they rejoiced exceedingly with great joy. And going into the house, they saw the child with Mary his mother, and they fell down and worshiped him. Then, opening their treasures, they offered him gifts, gold and frankincense and myrrh. And being warned in a dream not to return to Herod, they departed to their own country by another way.

O Come, All Ye Faithful
"Come and behold Him"

The English language has changed so much through the years. The years of people saying 'thus' and 'thither' have passed, and we have cycled into 'hard pass' and 'silver fox'. Actually these are two of the new phrases added to the dictionary in 2021, and next year newer words will be added.

Our language is constantly changing and morphing with the trends. Words and phrases of your grandparents are now long gone. Even words and phrases of a few years ago have already been deemed unhip and have been sent to your parents' vocabularies to eventually fade off into the distance.

There are many faith words that are said in scripture and inside the church walls, but are as used elsewhere as much as the words in an Elizabethan sonnet.

Words like 'exalted', 'holiness', 'sanctified', 'transgressions', and 'rend'. These are words we say from the pulpit but seldom speak in social settings over a cup of coffee or in a Tweet.

Another common church word that people hardly say outside of Sundays is 'behold'. What does this word mean?

Behold means to see or observe something, especially something remarkable or impressive.

When someone sees the breath-taking Grand Canyon, the snow-capped Rocky Mountains, or the rushing Niagara Falls, they are not likely to say 'behold'. But the word most certainly fits for all of these occasions.

I witnessed the Grand Canyon on my first adult vacation after college. I decided I was going to fly somewhere since I had never flown before and decided to head to Las Vegas because I was told it had a lot of things to see and it was inexpensive. During that trip I hopped on a bus and headed to the Grand Canyon. I remember walking toward the edge and feeling overwhelmed. I was overwhelmed by the enormity of the canyon in front of me and by the smallness of me.

There have been many moments in my life when I knew I was experiencing something worthy to behold. But environmental creations aren't the only things that cause that feeling.

Anything can be worthy of beholding if it is truly worthy, from the Great Pyramids, the Statue of Liberty, Wrigley Field, or your child. Everyone has a different measuring stick of saying something is worthy to behold.

In the beautiful Christmas hymn "O Come, All Ye Faithful," it is easy to get lost in the Christmas spirit and overlook the powerful message. The line that causes my knees to become weak like walking up the edge of the Grand Canyon is:

"Come and behold Him"

I love the simplicity of this phrase containing such a powerful meaning. When we sing the word 'come' it is an invitation for all of us. It doesn't matter your background or theology prowess, all are welcomed. All are said to come.

Christ didn't come for a select few. He came to redeem us all. He didn't pick and choose the cream of the crop or the godliest to be set apart. He came for the scoundrels cheating their way through life just as much as Mother Teresa. To Jesus, we are all the same. We are all lost in need of His grace and redemption.

When we are asked to come it isn't to just walk by and take a peek at God. It isn't a photo op for a selfie with the Maker of the world. It isn't some ordinary event like going out for dinner.

When we come we should behold Him.

We should look at Him like He is something remarkable and impressive. It should cause us to lose our breath when we catch a glimpse of Him. Our body should feel the magnitude of His sight.

When was the last time you felt like you were beholding Him?

When Christ was born, the shepherds felt the bewilderment. They felt the beholding power in the pastures as the angels covered the sky. They sought out this Messiah. They came and beheld Him.

We too should come and behold Him. Sometimes to feel like you are witnessing something that deserves to be beheld, you need to put it in perspective.

Did you create the world? No.

Did you raise the dead? No.

Do you cause the sun to rise every day? No.

Do you know how many stars are in the universe? No.

Is He worthy to behold? Yes.

But if you need more examples.

Did you create thousands of species of birds? No.

Did you create the language of DNA? No.

Did you form gravity? No.

Do you cause the tides? No.

You can spend your entire life listing the accomplishments of God and you would never repeat one item. Never.

Is He worthy to behold? Yes.

There is nothing that comes close to His worthiness. There is nothing that can even compare to His majesty. You can line up every great figure in history, monumental event, architectural wonder, and earthly wonder, but none can scratch the surface of God.

We all need to uncover the wonder of God a little more. None of us stand in awe of Him as much as He deserves.

May we all try to peel a layer to discover the true character of God. Not just the character that is recited on Sundays or prayer meetings, but the character we personally see and know. It is one thing to know about God, but it is something else to truly know Him. May we each know Him a little more. Then, little by little, our perspective and attitude toward God will change. We will see Him in a different light. We may even become blinded by His glory like Moses.

May we continue to dig into the scriptures and read His holy word with intrigue and devotion. May we continue to commune with God in our own personal way. May our prayer life and communication grow stronger. May our spirit start to intertwine more and more with His.

May we come and behold Him like He deserves.

Come and see what God has done:

he is awesome in his deeds toward the children of man. Psalm 66:5

You have multiplied, O Lord my God,

your wondrous deeds and your thoughts toward us;

None can compare with you!

I will proclaim and tell of them,

Yet they are more than can be told. Psalm 40:5

God,

    You are something to behold. Amen

O Come, O Come, Emmanuel
"Bid all our sad divisions cease"

In the Commonwealth of Kentucky, we have a motto, "United we stand, divided we fall." If we look throughout history we will see proof of this saying. Through the ages empires have fallen when another political party tried to rise within; corporations have crumbled or split when stockholders couldn't agree; and families have succumbed to the ugliness of taking sides.

History shows us divisions are not a new fad. There have always been divisions, even from Biblical times when kingdoms were split, families were divided, and livestock and land were separated. It is sad that though there are times when we have learned from our mistakes, history tends to be an ever-constant cycle of repetition.

I was recently reading an article that stated that even though people think we are more divided than ever, we actually agree on more than we realize. Yes, there are the hot topics that cause people's blood to boil when opposition is in sight, but if you look past some of these uncomfortable debatable notions, the world is more united than ever.

Yet sometimes people don't want to be united, especially when it's unity with their enemy.

I know there are some people who will always disagree with their nemesis. Their rival could say the grass is green, and they would still find a way to not agree with them out of spite. Sadly, these people are always going to be around. These people are always going to be stirring the pot to keep the friction going.

These people are the drama-lovers.

I know some of these people, and they can easily turn a mundane conversation into a war rally with some careful placements of key words and ideas. And if you are not careful, you, too, could be painting signs and picketing before you realize it.

When Jesus was born in the small town of Bethlehem there were divisions. The world was just as prejudiced, if not more, on religion, ethnicity, sex, and age. We hear the story of the Good Samaritan and think Jesus was teaching about helping someone in need. But the Jews hated the Samaritans. So even though the story was teaching about helping someone in need, it was also teaching of letting go of the divisions that have been passed down for generations.

When Jesus was traveling and teaching God's message of grace and love, he acquired a devout following. Many people followed him because he preached of a new kingdom, and the Jews hated being under Roman control -- another division held by the Jews. But Jesus wasn't speaking of an earthly kingdom, but a heavenly one. His followers were expecting him to rise in power and take down the evil Roman Empire.

But that wasn't how it went.

A few years later, after Jesus' death and resurrection, Paul, a newly converted follower of Christ, preached many times of divisions. He commanded the Church to be united. He urged the Church to respect the government (a government that was persecuting them). He pleaded for the Church to show love to one another and others.

You cannot show love and be divided.

"O Come, O Come, Emmanuel" is probably one of my favorite Christmas hymns. The melody of the first line of the hymn is hauntingly beautiful. When I hear the music of this hymn I can picture a group of monks singing this song in the dark ages. The melody lures me in each time I hear it. It takes me to another place and time. Isn't that what good music should do?

There are many lines in this hymn that need to be examined beyond the surface of their lyrics, but the line that stands out to me during this time is,

"Bid all our sad divisions cease"

I have never seen any happy divisions. Have you? Have you ever smiled when a friendship ended? Have you giggled after a gut-wrenching fight? Have you given a thumbs-up when a war breaks out? There is such a heaviness in divisions, and they take a toll in all aspects of our lives.

Jesus did not come to Earth to bring divisions. He came to show the need to end the conflicts, to end the bickering, to end the hatred that wedges deep into our souls.

He is called the Prince of Peace for a reason. He wasn't called the Duke of Division. I sometimes wonder what God is thinking when He sees His children screaming at one another. I do not think He would nod His head and enjoy the spiteful words of hate and degradation. I can't envision Him watching from His throne engrossed like watching a boxing match. I can't fathom Him being proud when we act like enemies instead of family.

We will never agree on everything. The early followers of Christ who witnessed His miracles and walked where He walked didn't agree with one another all the time. There are many accounts where they disagreed, even in Jesus' presence. But Jesus never let them stay separated. He would take that moment and teach them. He wouldn't let them simmer in their dislike, but He would show them the error of their ways.

We may not always agree, but that doesn't give us reason to be divided. I have seen adults disagree and part ways after years of friendship. I have also seen adults disagree and remain faithful friends. They may not see eye-to-eye on some topics, but they know they will always have each other's backs.

We are the body of Christ. We each have a different part, a different skill, a different talent, maybe a different viewpoint, but our differences shouldn't divide us. Our differences should make us stronger. I may never be able to reach the Hollywood billionaires and share Christ with them, just as someone else may not be able to build a relationship with a tribe in the Congo. It takes different people to fulfill the law of Christ.

But our differences shouldn't divide us. They should unify us.

May we sing this hymn and hold the hand of someone we once disagreed with. May we go to our enemy and humbly apologize for words said in anger and haste. May we raise the next generation to show through our actions that love is stronger than hate. May we continue to show the love of Christ even to those who hate us.

We are not called to share the greatest gift with just our friends and family. We are commanded to share the gift of grace with our

Samaritans we have ignored, with our Romans who stand over us, with our Gentiles who mock us, with our Pharisees who ridicule us, with our friends and family who have betrayed us.

The world will always be divided, but we don't have to be one of the reasons for the division. We can be a living example for a solution.

I appeal to you, brothers, by the name of our Lord Jesus Christ, that all of you agree, and that there be no divisions among you, but that you be united in the same mind and the same judgment. 1 Corinthians 1:10

A new command I give to you, that you love one another; just as I have loved you, you also are to love one another. John 13:34

God,

Help me to forgive as You have forgiven me. Amen

Good Christian Men, Rejoice
"Jesus Christ was born for this"

Have you asked yourself recently, "Why was I born?" The question doesn't have to be one of depression-laden angst with a woeful mentality, but one of hopeful resolution and optimism. I sometimes wonder about my purpose here on Earth.

I have seen my plan change through the years. When I was younger I had certain dreams and plans, but they morphed into other dreams and plans. And then those evolved into something new and different as well.

Do we really have a specific purpose or plan? Or should that mentality be the same across the board? Shouldn't all of our goals be to share the love of Christ? Shouldn't our ultimate ambition be to spread the love of Christ to everyone we meet? Shouldn't that be our greatest accomplishment?

But God created us all differently. He created some of us with skills I will never be able to achieve. He crafted some of us with talents that far exceed my loftiest dreams. He grafted some of us with characteristics I can only dare to imagine.

The God of creativity created us all uniquely different but with the same endgame in mind. Isn't that amazing?

It doesn't seem possible to make each individual person unique, even after all of the billions that have been on this planet of ours, but He did. There are no duplicates. There are no carbon copies. There are no manufactured presses of Erics that produce a hundred of me in a day. We are all "fearfully and wonderfully made."

That is what I find fascinating. Even though we are so different with our outward and inward appearances, we are all made in God's image. Even though some of us have blonde hair, or dark skin, or slanted eyes, or one arm, we were all created to look the way we look to fulfill the mission given to each of us. The mission to share the love of Christ with every man.

I may never be able to impress someone with my theatrics, but maybe God instilled that talent with you to use it for His glory. And I may never be able to wow a crowd with three-pointers or foul shots, but maybe God planned for you to use it for His glory.

You may think God cannot use your gifts and talents, but what if the very reason you have those skills is because He created you to use them for His glory? What if you were made the way you were to share His love to the world through the use of your passion and dreams?

'What if' is a pretty big question when God is involved.

"Good Christian Men Rejoice" conveys to me the sound of a military anthem. The beat and the tone sound like a march we would see in a parade with a military procession.

There are many lovely lines in this Christmas hymn, but the one that stands out the loudest to me is probably one of the lines that seems the most familiar during the Christmas season:

"Jesus Christ was born for this"

You may wonder why I picked this line to analyze, but if someone had never heard the Christmas story or even the name of Jesus, this line may evoke question upon question.

"What was He born for?" they may ask. "What makes Him so special?" someone else may ponder.

Just as God created each of us for a divine purpose He planned before the dawn of time, He sent Jesus for a specific purpose.

The Gospels are full of stories of the teachings and miracles of Jesus, but if Jesus had lived to the ripe old age of ninety-nine and then died peacefully in his sleep, He would not have fulfilled His purpose. Jesus wasn't born to give us an intriguing biography full of mesmerizing miracles like when He fed thousands of people with a few pieces of bread and fish. He wasn't born to showcase His magician-like raising of the dead or causing the lame to walk. He wasn't born to share His teachings and wisdom that confounded the wise and silenced the jealous. Even though He did all of these things, His purpose was for something greater.

It is humbling to consider His purpose from birth was to be a sacrificial lamb. From the moment He breathed His first breath, He was ready to start His journey to the cross of Calvary. It is a little haunting to think that while Mary and Joseph were cuddling their new son in Bethlehem, the angels were witnessing the start of a path they knew He would walk.

The angels may not have known all the details that would come thirty-three years later, but they knew His purpose. They knew Jesus came as the Messiah for the dark and lost world.

If we consider the Christmas season as the start of a long journey toward death, it seems very heavy with despair. But ultimately, that is what Christmas is. It is the momentous birth of the precious Lamb of God sent to be slain for the sins of all humanity.

When we say we feel the weight of the world on our shoulders we cannot fathom the load Jesus had to carry for His life — a load where He had to stay pure and sinless. A weight where one wrong move or tiptoe into temptation would cause the fate of everyone to unravel. It was a heaviness that each step He took was one step closer to the final path of His death.

Jesus Christ was born for this!

He was born to redeem us from our deathly debt. He was born to restore us to the Father. He was born to reconcile our unbalanced life to the perfection of His. He was born to remove the blemishes we could not wash away ourselves. He was born to restore the Father's plan for an eternity of community with Him.

He was born to be ridiculed and scoffed in each of our places.

He was born to be marred and beaten in each of our places.

He was born to be tortured and mocked in each of our places.

He was born to be crucified and killed in each of our places.

And then the story shifted. It flipped upside down. It changed, and the whole world stopped. Everything that had been leading to this point of Jesus Christ's death suddenly was split like the curtain in the temple. All that was known was instantaneously made complete. All the missing holes were suddenly filled. All the puzzle pieces started to fall into place. All the confusing stories stopped swirling and halted in a peaceful resolution.

Jesus Christ was born for His resurrection. He was born to defeat death. He was born to graft us to the Father once and for all. He was born to end the battle.

Jesus Christ was born for this!

If that isn't a beautiful line that is often overlooked, I don't know what is.

But he was pierced for our transgressions,

he was crushed for our iniquities;

upon him was the chastisement that brought us peace,

and with his wounds we are healed. Isaiah 53:5

But when the fullness of time had come, God sent forth his Son, born of woman, born under the law, to redeem those who were under the law, so that we might receive adoption as sons. Galatians 4:4-5

God,

Thank you for being born for me. Amen

The First Noel the Angel Did Say
"and to follow the star wherever it went"

'Noel' is a beautiful word. The way it rolls off the tongue just sounds more appealing than 'Christmas' to my ears. The two words have the same number of syllables, but the softness of the letters of 'Noel' seems to comfort me like a wool blanket in front of a frosted windowpane. Call me strange, but 'Noel' is just a refreshing word. If I started a trend of saying 'Merry Noel', I don't think it would catch on. I may not be the first to ever say 'Merry Noel', but I'm the first one that I know who has thought of it.

There are many firsts. With everything you do, there is always a first. You may not remember them all, but if you are doing something now, there must have been a time when you did it for the first time. Not all firsts are good or pleasing, but even if they are bad they are sometimes still remembered. First loves are often followed by first jilted hearts. First jobs can also come with first layoffs. First successes also come with first declines. But the opposite is also true. First dashed hopes can spark first skyrocketing fireworks. First falls could bring about first recoveries.

Just because something may be bad at first, doesn't mean it has to stay bad. Your attitude determines a majority of your future. If you feel like your first attempt is going to be a failure, are you going to try it? If you feel like your first shot is going to be an air ball, are you going to give it your best? If you feel like your first go is going to flop, you may never actually flop because you were too afraid to go in the first place.

Don't let the fear of your first time stop a path of seconds, thirds, fourths, and so on. You have to squash that fear before it becomes the inner voice you listen to and follow all the time.

We've all had many failures on our first attempts. As a toddler, did you stop trying to walk because you fell on your first try? As a kid did you stop trying to catch a ball because you missed it on the first throw? Did you stop trying to ride a bike because you fell off on your first attempt without training wheels? Think of what a miserable life you would be living if you never tried anything new.

No savoring a candy bar. No devouring a Hawaiian pizza. No road trips decided by a dart and a map. If you never tried anything new, you would still be slurping milk while lying on your back as a grown adult. Firsts can be scary, but they are essential. Without firsts you may never have found your love of painting, or tennis, or the blonde you have called your wife for the last ten years. Firsts may cause butterflies in your stomach, but I would rather have a flurry of swarming wings beating inside me than a herd of crawling caterpillars too afraid to take a chance.

We can be a generation of change or doing the same old thing as the prior generation. There is nothing wrong with tradition, but why use an abacus when you can use a calculator? Why chart your course looking up at the stars when you can program the address into a GPS? Why settle for the satisfaction of yesteryears when you can explore the dreams of tomorrow?

The line that stands out in "The First Noel the Angel Did Say" that spurs me is,

Many times in life we look up to those that lead. We find respect in the courage of someone commanding their troops; we promote the souls that can see beyond the mundane; we campaign for ones that we hope to make the world better. We follow politicians and rock stars, liking their tweets and Instagram pics for no other reason than because of who they are. We see them as leaders, and we revere that characteristic as being better than a follower.

But weren't all leaders at first followers?

I seriously doubt Alexander the Great woke up one morning and decided to expand his territory without any advice or training. I cannot see Albert Einstein discovering all of his scientific findings without first being taught mathematics and science. I cannot see anyone in history who was born a leader, because everyone is ultimately born a follower. But I have seen many born followers choose to become leaders.

What are you following?

You can ask any leader in the world and they will tell you someone they admire, respect, or follow in one way or another. The only difference between them being a leader and a follower is the person who follows them. There can be many great followers with great ideas to charge a way, but if they don't have anyone to instruct they will remain in the shadow of someone else.

Shadows are interesting if you think about it. Depending on where the light is coming from will determine the length of a shadow. If a light is directly overhead, the shadow will not travel very far because it will fall directly underneath the thing it is shadowing. But if the direction of the light changes, if it shines from the side and lowers, the shadow will elongate and travel until the light itself fades into nothing. A shadow is only as strong as the light that makes it.

In the Biblical account of the wise men following the star, they traveled from the East until they reached Bethlehem finding Jesus. Who is the leader in this story? Is the star the leader and the wise men the followers, or was one wise man a leader and the other travelers the followers?

The wise men followed the light from the star, but we have the light of the world to follow now since Christ came to Earth. We have a perfect example to follow. We have a light that shines through the ages, casting our shadow to places we could never dream. The light is already shining in those dark places. We just have to take that first step toward the light and follow where it goes. We may not leave a tattoo on the world, but for a brief moment in time, we are leaving a shadow if we are standing in the light.

But many people confuse the light of the world for the light of their world. They follow the flickering flame of prestige in hopes of casting a shadow on all of their constituents. People follow the flashy sparkler that will die out in thirty seconds so they can embrace their small dose of fame. We live in a generation of people bartering their eternal souls for makeshift blocks of gold in order to have the Midas touch for a day, not worrying about the ramifications of their poor decisions.

When we look for a neon sign showing a vacancy, we often end up in situations that will swallow us up and spit us back out. When we find the loopholes or the easy ways out, we often find out they were not the easy ways after all with all of their catches and strings attached.

May we learn to be a generation that follows the light of the world no matter where He leads. God doesn't guarantee an easy life with neatly packaged presents and silky bows. Nowhere in the Bible does God say to follow him and everything is going to be rainbows and ice cream sundaes. No where in faith does it say life is going to be without any bumps in the road. God may have planned for us to live like this in Eden, but then humanity stumbled. But once Adam and Eve left the bounty of the garden, God warned them of the hardships they would endure.

Following God doesn't guarantee success in man's eyes, but it does guarantee success in His. You may fall flat on your face in front of your friends and family, but even Christ fell as He was carrying the cross. Following His light may not be easy, but it is the path He ordained for us as He was breathing out stars. He has a plan for your life that is good. A plan for your life to follow.

So are you going to follow and cast a lifelong shadow from His light?

Or are you going to try to lead and leave nothing behind but a fleeting shadow from your own light?

In all your ways acknowledge Him, and He will make straight your paths. Proverbs 3:6

My sheep hear my voice, and I know them, and they follow me. John 10:27

God,

Lead me and help me follow. Amen

It Came upon the Midnight Clear
"O rest beside the weary road"

There is so much beauty in a cloudless night. In summer evenings I love to lie in my driveway and look up at the stars. I sometimes wish I knew more of what I was looking at, but I can at least pick out the two Dippers. But not knowing the stars' names or which twinkling lights make up the constellations doesn't minimize the beauty. You don't have to understand something to lie in amazement of it.

That is the astonishment of beautiful things; an art historian and a punk teenager can both look at a statue carved by Michelangelo and stand in awe of its beauty. Beauty draws us all in no matter where we are from. It is the great equalizer.

There is so much in this world that is ugly. Not just an ugliness in physical appearance, but in shock value, rudeness, egotism, hatred, and division. However, there is a sweet feeling to breathe a sigh of relief and forget about the drama that seems to ebb its way into our hearts. Some of the best memories at Christmas time are those quiet nights after the television has been turned off and the only things on are the lights from the Christmas tree giving off their beautiful glow. It's in those quiet moments that my heart breathes a sigh of relief. It may not be flashy or showy, but these are the beautiful moments in life to sit before the lights and feel a sense of peace.

There is so much beauty in the feeling of peace. I wonder if that is why I feel a longing to stare up at the black sky and gaze upon the heavenly lights to find that feeling of peace that eludes me through the day. To look up at the great expanse above that stretches from east to west as far as I can see. It is in those moments of solitude that I feel humbled. When life is going haywire and I start to focus all my time and energy on myself, it is easy to get sucked into that whirlpool of only looking at myself. Watching my own back. Making sure I have what I need. Deciding what is best for me.

But when I lie under the stars, I realize I am not the center of everything. I am not the sun. And then as I stare up at the heavens a little longer I remember the sun isn't in the middle of everything. It is only in the middle of our little solar system, which is a dot in the Milky Way Galaxy, which is an even tinier dot in the entire universe.

We may think that without us life would cease to exist, but the only thing that is going to stop existing once we are gone is ourselves. The world is going to keep going. Our loved ones may grieve for a period, but their lives will continue. It may not continue the way they like, but the world will not come to a halt when we take our last breath. All the tragedies in the world that have come before never caused the world to stop. It may have rattled people to their core, but the world kept spinning.

An old Christmas carol that I don't hear too often, "It Came upon the Midnight Clear", has a stunningly beautiful line that we all need to hear:

"O rest beside the weary road"

You may wonder why we are singing about a weary road in a Christmas carol, but I think this line is pertinent because we all have weary roads. There are days that are ugly with rude customers, backstabbing co-workers, hateful clients, disgruntled employers, back-talking kids, and sudden heartbreaks. It is easy to want to run and hide away on days of walking the weary road. You may have been walking a weary road for days or weeks or maybe even years. I am deeply sorry for the road you have walked.

I am an optimist. I try my hardest to spin any lemon in life into a glass of sugary lemonade. I try to squeeze the storm clouds and pop out a rainbow. I try to see every coin toss as a positive.

But sometimes it is okay to just take a break and rest. Some of my favorite stories in the Bible are when Jesus was consoling those who were hurting. He didn't brush away their pain with a fake smile. He didn't douse them with a bottle of good tidings and push them on their way. He didn't pretend there wasn't any ugliness in the world.

In fact, I think Jesus saw the ugliness of the world much clearer than anyone else. He heard the words said to women in the marketplace. He witnessed the downcast looks of the lepers begging for a touch. He saw the arrogant noses turn a blind eye to the poor and needy. He came face to face with those clinging to their last thread.

But He also knew what no one else knew. He knew the hearts of everyone around Him. He knew the thoughts of doubt that followed Him as they were mixed among the faithful crowd. Yet He also knew the motives in the crowds' actions in their needs for selfish prayers answered. He read the minds of backstabbers and so-called friends. He foresaw the outcomes that the deniers didn't want to see. He saw the ugliness in each man and woman's heart. He saw the corrosion of sin that was covered with perfumed robes. He knew the darkness that feasted upon every man's heart.

And He still knows.

And He still doesn't pass over our weary roads like a crosswalk. No, He stops and rests beside us. He offers us His hand to hold and His shoulder to lean on. He doesn't give up when the going gets tough, and He never abandons us when all our friends have scurried away. He doesn't point out our flaws, but touches our wounds mercifully and shows us a new direction. But He doesn't force us to move. He doesn't push us from the nest. He doesn't belittle the baby steps of faith. He meets us where we are and waits.

Your weary road may be at the bottom of a bottle. He's not judging your drunken stupor. Your weary road may be in the arms of another lover. He's not judging your loveless actions. Your weary road may be with a line of white powder. He's not judging your misguided outlet. Your weary road may be a cutting razor blade. He's not judging your need for a relief. Your weary road may be restless nights in bed. He's not judging your self-torment.

Even though those weary roads are destructive, He still finds you where you are. God roams the halls of every prison just as He roams the halls of my prisoner's heart. There is no place that His light cannot shine. You may not see His light shining, but it is. It may just be a flicker, a flint, a tiny spark, but His light is too powerful to be extinguished. Nothing can separate you from His light.

We all have a weary road. But you don't have to walk it alone. Put down that bottle. Get out of that bed. Flush away those drugs. Bandage up your arm. Look in the mirror and see a ray of hope. If you don't see it, ask someone who can point it out to you. Then ask another. And another. And another.

Fan that flame until you can see it.

But if you are tired, just rest for a while. And then try tomorrow. There is nothing wrong with resting. It's only wrong when you give up. Resting is not giving up. Resting is gearing up to fight another day.

So take a deep breath. And then take another. And then take another. It doesn't matter how many deep breaths you take as long as it leads you closer to taking another step.

And when you are ready, you don't have to walk the weary road alone. Life is about finding a hand to hold in the hard moments. It is about locking elbows with another to spur one another on. It is about grabbing a shoulder when you need a crutch. It is about whispering hopeful words into one another's ears when the weary road looks too hard.

Because the weary road isn't that hard. It is just like all the other roads.

But one of the best things about the weary roads is those are the roads where you can feel Jesus walking beside you the most. It is not that He doesn't walk beside you on all the other roads, but we tend to ignore His presence in the straight paths, the beachfront walkways, the cozy sidewalks, and the landscaped driveways because we don't feel like we need to lean on His eternal strength when life is going well. He is still walking beside us on those journeys, but sadly, we miss His touch because we are not reaching out for it.

But when we walk on the gravel roads that may trip us, we reach out for help. Those are the moments that we feel Him closest because we take our eyes off of ourselves and look toward Him.

I have a love-hate relationship with the weary roads. I hate them when life is going lovely. I hate the feeling of being pressed and broken. But sometimes we have to be broken to be made better than ever. I hate the feeling of brokenness, but I love to feel His touch when He's mending. I may hate the weary roads when I'm walking through them, but my history of weary roads is one I would never want to erase. It's in those low paths that I felt His love and mercy the most. It's in those weary roads when I felt His rest. It's in those deserted roads that I finally knew I wasn't deserted because He was with me. He was always with me.

May we learn to feel His touch this Christmas season when we see the beauty. But if you are seeing the ugliness, reach out. He's there.

Come to me, all you who are weary and burdened, and I will give you rest. Take my yoke upon you and learn from me, for I am gentle and humble in heart, and you will find rest for your souls. For my yoke is easy and my burden is light. Matthew 11:28-30 NIV

In peace I will lie down and sleep,
for you alone, Lord,
make me dwell in safety. Psalm 4:8 NIV

God,

Walk with me on the weary and not-so-weary roads. Amen

I Heard the Bells on Christmas Day
"God is not dead, nor doth He sleep"

Do you hear bells on Christmas Day? There are some traditions that have phased out through the years, but some churches still have a bell to chime on Christmas morning. Today most church bells are rung on timers, so there aren't actual people pulling on the ropes to announce to the world it's Christmas Day. But there's something picturesque when I hear church bells ringing and I can envision someone standing below the bell, gripping the rope and pulling down to create the beautiful sound to echo through the city streets.

There are many other traditions that we have left behind. Some were good to be left behind like bell bottoms and 80's hairstyles, but some important traditions are missing in society today. There was a time when nothing was open on Sundays. Can you imagine a Sunday where restaurants and shopping centers are all closed? Where would we eat? We would have to actually have a family dinner around our tables at home. Perish the thought! We have moved past treating Sunday as a day of rest to seeing it as a day like any other.

I remember when I was kid, counting down to the end of the school year, ready for summer break. I remember vividly a time sitting in my elementary cafeteria thinking that high school seemed so far away. I smile now at how wrong I was as it seems time continues to go by faster the older I get. Times have changed; some changes are good and some are bad.

The world seems to be a more violent place with terrorist attacks, or maybe we are just more aware with the daily newsfeeds in the age of texts and cell phones; yet we also live in a world where freedom is attainable in areas where it wasn't decades ago. We live in the age of medical advancements that have helped increase the average lifespan, but it also seems we hear of more incidents of cancer and heart disease. We live in the generation that preconceived notions of your family history can be overlooked if you have the determination to make something of yourself. But on the other side of the coin, your family history is sometimes a curse that seldom is broken, which causes a domino effect to the next generation.

There are moments I wish we could rewind the clocks and go back to a simpler time, but is simpler always better?

Would you rather hear the bells on Christmas Day or the heartbeat of your unborn child through a sonogram?

There are many things that have changed through the sands of time, but there are some things as constant as the sunrise.

I have grown to love the Christmas carol, "I Heard the Bells on Christmas Day". This is another one of the carols that tells a beautiful poetic story intertwining uplifting and sorrowful lyrics into one carol. A line that is stunningly simplistic, yet powerful is,

"God is not dead, nor doth He sleep"

Speaking of things that have not changed, that line is one of them. God isn't dead. God is still God. He isn't taking a break. He hasn't stepped away from us and allowed us to wreak havoc on Earth. He is still present, even when we don't see Him. He is still among us, even if we can't hear Him. He is still working, even if we don't believe it.

It seems there has been a growing trend in the last generation to walk away from faith and claim atheism. When questions and doubts start to outweigh the scales of faith, soon no answer is good enough to salvage that mustard seed of faith you once had years ago. I find it disheartening to hear many intellectual minds state that believing in a higher being is like believing in a fairy tale. Many secular intellectuals have claimed the church has brainwashed people into believing, while the church states the same type of brainwashing is used on students at colleges and universities.

I wish I could prove to everyone that God is not dead, that He isn't a fabricated story concocted by scared people needing to believe in something beyond themselves. I wish I could show proof to answer every one of their questions, but I can't. To be honest, I can't answer all of my questions either. So, if I can't answer all of my questions, how I can rationally answer all of someone else's?

I can't. I can't answer in complete certainty the deep theological questions that have been debated since the days of Christ. All I can do is question them myself. But at the end of the questioning, I have to rest in the sentiment of this song: "God is not dead, nor doth he sleep."

I would love to know all the philosophical questions that cause paradoxes and have spellbound millions before me, but I know I never will. Even though I don't know them, I still know something that no one else knows.

I can recall the moments when I felt God near me when no one else was around. I can go back in my memory and think of the times when I needed God and He showed up. I can list miracles I have seen that are beyond medical explanation. I can point out moments when God revealed Himself to me and then was verified by an outside source. I can go back to the nights of prayer when I felt the spirit move me in the right direction. I can open my Bible and remember incidents where the Word spoke louder than any other voice. I can close my eyes and go back to those moments, and when I do, all my fears vanish. All my questions and doubts fall away. All my demands for proof become insignificant because I have been shown proof many times before.

I can say with complete certainty that God is not dead because of the moments when He was alive with me. I may not be able to prove to anyone else that God is not dead, but He has already proven Himself to me many times before.

One of God's greatest gifts or curses, depending on how you look, is our memory. There are things that I never want to forget, but then there are some things I wish I could. The haunting of my failures may never be erased, but maybe it will teach me to make a wise decision in my future. You can live with regret, but don't let your regret determine your future. Use that regret to chart a course to better yourself.

The Old Testament is full of stories of regret. But the Hebrew children never swept their failures under the rug. They never cast them aside and pretended like they didn't happen. They didn't showcase their successes and minimize their defeats. They recorded the good and bad just the same. The Psalms are a beautiful example of this. There are Psalms where the writer pleads to God for forgiveness for wandering, and then there are Psalms where the writer praises God for His deliverance. The Psalms are like daily journal entries recalling the best and worst moments of their lives. But in each one, the psalmist knew who they were praising. They never had to second-guess if God was truly God. They knew.

So, if your life is hanging by a thread, ring a bell and listen to that heavenly tune. If your day was superb with accolades, ring a bell and praise the Heavenly Father. If your month has been filled with stress to the max, ring a bell and let go of what's holding you down. If your season has been full of high-fives and jobs-well-done, then ring a bell and press on for more blessings. If your year hasn't been like you planned, ring a bell and hold tight with faith for a better future. If your year has exceeded your expectations, ring a bell and share your rewards with others. If your life hasn't been what you dreamed, then ring a bell and dream with the God who dreams big dreams. If your life has exceeded your expectations, then ring a bell and dream with the God who dreams bigger dreams.

May you find comfort in the arms of a God who is fully alive and who is watching over you now. May you rest deeper into His lap, sinking into His loving embrace like a loving father. May you find solace in your pain and find hope for an abundant future. May you find rest in a relationship with the One who never rests. May you turn to Him in all seasons and occasions, since He is always ready and waiting for you to come. May you ring that bell proudly knowing that God is with you now and forever.

The Lord is near to all who call on Him,

to all who call on Him in truth. Psalm 145:18

The Lord is near to the brokenhearted

and saves the crushed in spirit. Psalm 34:18

God,

Remind me You are still here. Amen

God Rest Ye Merry, Gentlemen
"To free all those who trust in Him"

Are gentlemen merry? I tend to think women are merrier than men, but that may be a little sexist. There are some men who appear merry as they decorate the outside of their homes with festive lights, or deck themselves out with ugly Christmas sweaters and ties, or stand outside in the cold and deep-fry their Christmas turkey. But the majority of men I see do not get merry over Christmas. Or maybe they do and they just don't show it.

No matter our gender we should all be merry this time of year. Technically, we should be merry all year long for what Christ has done for us. We should greet one another daily with a warm smile, friends and strangers alike. We should show kindness and warm well-wishes to everyone we meet. We should show love to our neighbor – all our neighbors around the world.

Jesus was adamant we are to love every man. We are to show compassion to those on the other side of the political spectrum. We are to be cordial to those that bad mouth us to our face and behind our backs. We are to pray for those that persecute us.

I think I can be cordial and wear a smile to my enemy's face, but to speak to God on behalf of my enemies? Well, that takes a lot more self-control and Christ-like attitude.

I have been fortunate that I have not faced persecution like so many believers around the world. I do not have to worry about getting attacked for the Bible app on my phone or blindsided and thrown in the back of a van for my religious affiliations. I have never had to worry about saying the name of Christ. Should that sentiment bring a warmth to my heart? Or should it bring a chill?

If I was born in a different country and raised in a different religion, would I have turned to Christ when I heard of His salvation story? Or would I call the story a hoax? Would I be like the majority of the world and stick to my home-grown traditional beliefs and ignore the story a kind missionary spoke to me? Would I turn away from my family and follow this supposed Christ, even though it may guarantee persecution and untimely death?

Sadly, I do not know.

I do not know what I would do, because even though I have researched other religions to see what they believe, I have never truly dug into them for faith reasons. It was more for intellectual reasons to understand other religious foundations. But that goes to my underlying thought that since I am so grounded in my belief, would I be swayed if I was born a Buddhist?

Maybe I should count myself lucky to be raised in the Bible Belt. But even in the United States, there are many people who have a secular mindset. How can I ask them to consider a faith in Christ when I haven't considered a life without faith in Christ? Is that hypocritical? Is it false to assume your idea of faith is correct without looking at all the other ideas of faith out there?

This can lead to a slippery slope since there are many different religions, but the only saving grace I have is studying a book cannot deny my past experiences of a faith in Christ. I don't have to search for meaning through the Koran because I have found meaning in Christ. But how can we expect someone else to?

A line in the upbeat "God Rest Ye Merry, Gentlemen" that deserves some reflection is,

"To free all those who trust in Him"

I wish I could show people they are not free. I wish I could show them they do not have the freedom I have. But some people cannot see they are not free. And then there are other people who would say I am not free.

As followers of Christ, we are not guaranteed an easy existence. We are not warranted to receive all our dreams and plans in life. We are not all destined for anything more than to be called the sons and daughters of God. But we should live like we have something the others don't. We should live like we are free.

We should have a smile that draws people into our lives. We should have an attitude that compels people to question what makes us different. We should have an outlook that causes other people to want to follow us. We should have the hope in our Savior that we are free, now and forever.

But how many of us live our lives like this? How many times do you snap at a coworker that has annoyed you for the tenth time? How many times do you flip off someone who has cut you off in traffic a few minutes after leaving the church parking lot? How many times do your curse your enemies instead of bless them?

Why would someone who doesn't believe in Christ want to learn about this man who has supposedly freed His followers of their sins when all the believers look like they are still shackled?

Someone gave me an analogy years ago that stuck. Would you rather drink a new Coca-Cola that hasn't been opened, or would you rather drink one that was opened a week ago? The new beverage is crisp and sweet, full of flavor and vigor. The bottle opened last week has gone flat and stale. Which would you rather drink?

We should be like the new, unopened bottle. When people talk to us they should hear that pop in our voice so full of life. When people come to us with a dilemma they should feel a vibrancy and warmth. In a world of hate, depression, unbalance, anxiousness, rage, badness, faithlessness, harshness, and self-centeredness, we need to show them there is something more.

There is one who can replace the hate with love. There is a savior who gives joy in the middle of depression. There is a prince who gives unfathomable peace in the unbalance. There is a counselor who gives patience to the anxious. There is a healer who gives kindness to those filled with rage. There is a father who gives goodness when all they see is badness. There is a friend who is more faithful than anyone else. There is a great physician who gives gentleness in the harsh times. There is a sacrificial lamb who shows self-control in a self-centered society.

I wish we could be a people who could show the world what true freedom looks like: denying ourselves and trusting Him with every aspect of our lives.

Some people would see self-denial as surrender and weakness, but that is the glorious news of the Gospels -- what may sound ludicrous is actually perfectly sound. With Christ, the weak are made strong, the lost are found, the blind can see, the deaf can hear, and the dead can live again. What confounds the wise doesn't confound the followers of Christ.

May we show the merry side of ourselves this Christmas season and may it seep into all times of the year. May our freedom cause others to ask questions, cause them to ponder, cause them to seek, cause them to want what we have. Then we can show them that freedom is trusting not in ourselves who will forever let us down, but trusting in the One who will never abandon or forsake us. When we follow Christ we have to pick up our cross and follow Him, but the interesting thing is, He has already carried the heaviest load. When we follow Him, we are not walking alone. We are walking with Him and the other believers with us who are spurring us on, encouraging us, and helping us.

Freedom doesn't mean walking alone. Freedom means walking with someone greater than ourselves. It may be hard to trust Him with your life, but your life will be so much better if you do.

May we all walk with our backs a little straighter knowing we are free. May our walk cause others to notice. Then as we follow, may we share the love of Christ so they, too, can walk a little easier.

Trust in the Lord with all your heart,
and do not lean on your own understanding. Proverbs 3:5

And those who know your name put their trust in you,

for you, O Lord, have not forsaken those who seek you. Psalm 9:10

God,

Thank you for freeing me. Amen

The Little Drummer Boy
"I have no gift to bring"

I love presents. I don't really care much about getting presents, but I like to give them. I like to see the expression on my loved ones' faces when they realize that I thought about them and wanted to get them something special. When I saw that sweater on the rack, I thought of them. Or I knew they liked Arby's so I got them a gift card. People may think some presents are not very thoughtful, but I see it as someone taking time, even if only a few minutes. That is a few minutes that someone could have been doing something else other than thinking of you.

But Christmas has become very commercialized. There is nothing wrong with buying presents, but if you are only buying a present for someone because it's the thing to do, then that's the wrong thing to do. Christmas is a time to show love to your neighbors. It is a time to embrace the world and hope for a better future. It is a season to give of your blessings to those who may need one.

I am truly blessed. When I look around the shops there is nothing I desire. Some may call me spoiled, and technically that may be true, but I prefer to be called blessed. God has blessed me with the things I need. God has granted me the things I don't really need. He has supplied my wants up to a level and has given me contentment for the things I do not have. I wish I could say my contentment level will be enough to get me through this life and buying a tangible object never brings me happiness, but I know that is where the spoiled me comes in and surprises myself with a little delight.

I wrestle with the notion of the line between blessed and spoiled. Compared to the majority of the world I would consider myself spoiled for having a nice roof over my head, running water in my faucet, a soft, warm bed to sleep in each night, and a refrigerator stocked with food to eat at midnight when I get hungry. When do my blessings become my spoils?

I speak with friends on this idea every once in a while. Is there an amount of giving in donations and charities that will ever satisfy my desire to do enough? Will I ever reach that point in my checkbook where I have given all I am able to? Will I ever reach a point where I can clock out on my volunteer efforts, wipe my hands, and say I have done enough?

I think when we believe we have done enough is the day we need to re-evaluate ourselves. There shouldn't be a day we should stop and say we have nothing else to give. Even if you are down to your last penny, you are not down to your last minute. Even if you are down to your last minute, you are not down to your last talent. Even if you think you have nothing to give, there is always something else.

Love is probably the best gift because it's something no one else can give. Other people can give their love, but they can never give your love. That is one of the few things that can never be unmatched.

I know I have already used this Christmas carol, and even though it is not one of my favorite carols musically, it is one of my favorites symbolically. One of my favorite lines in "The Little Drummer Boy" is,

Have you ever tried to give a present to someone who has everything? Have you wracked your brain, scurried through Amazon at midnight, and come up with a genius idea only to wake up the next morning realizing it was not so genius? It was only a genius idea at midnight when you should have been sleeping.

I have a hard time buying presents for people in my family. We all have so much and we don't need anything. If we need anything we buy it. If we want to treat ourselves, we splurge when the item goes on sale.

But even though I have such a hard time finding the best present for them, I still try to find something that will bring them some joy. I try to think of something that will bring a smile to their face even if I find out later they already have it. But mostly, I want my family to know I love them and would do anything for them, even if it is to buy a measly gift card so they can get exactly what they want.

So, this Christmas season what have you gotten God?

Yeah, God. The creator of the universe. The maker of every tree that is planted in the Amazon and the carver of every mountainside in the Alps. What present could ever be enough?

I think that is why I love the story behind the song "Little Drummer Boy" so much. Even though I am blessed beyond my expectations, I am a penniless little kid compared to the glorious riches of my God and King. Even though I can buy the so-called desires of my envious heart, I cannot buy the desires of my Sovereign Lord.

So, what does God want for Christmas?

Another question may be, what does God want from me every day?

The scripture can be summed up with two rules to follow: love God and love man. I think that is what God wants for Christmas. I think He wants nothing else than for us to see Him for who He truly is and love Him for that. I wonder if He wants us to shut down our phones for some time and think about Him. To sit and think of the many ways we can show God our love and devotion.

We can pray and talk to God like a friend over a cup of coffee and a sugar cookie. We can listen for His still small and wise voice. We can drink in his words through the reading of the Bible. We can let the words simmer in our hearts until it blends into our entire being like a peppermint mocha. We can reflect upon the meanings and let the power of the Holy Spirit ignite a passion on our soul hotter and more powerful than a piping cup of coffee. We can sing to Him a new song or an old favorite. We can praise Him by creating or by allowing His love to create something new in us.

But we can't overlook the second thing we are commanded to do – to love one another.

This may be easier for most since we can actually see one another. But it can also be much harder.

Is there an olive branch you need to give? Is there a reconciliation that needs to take place? Are you harboring some ill-will this season thinking, "God bless us everyone, except her?" Is there someone's face lurking in your memory as you read these lines with the words you shouted or texted back and forth to one another?

It may be hard, but there is no better time of year to reconcile than the Christmas season. You may never be best friends through the years of wear and damage, but you can be civil and wish good tidings to them. It may be awkward to confront the person from your past, but it will do you some good.

Forgiveness is a two-way road. The more you give it, the more you are healed as well. It is funny how forgiveness is one of the few things that as you give it, it comes back. I'm not saying the other person will forgive you for the damages you may have done, but it's cleansing to purge the gunk out of your life and start fresh.

God wants us to love everyone, even those we don't like. He has never said, "It's okay that you don't like him, because I know what he did to you."

Would you want God to say that to you? I'm fairly certain you have done much worse things to God than that old boyfriend or backstabbing best friend from the seventh grade. None of us are flawless. We have all burned bridges. We have all caused wedges in relationships and walked away as if leaving the scene of a crime.

God has seen all the corrupt things we have done, and yet He still loves us. If God can love us despite our flaws, the very least we can do is love the ones we are called to love. I don't know everything you have done, just as I don't know everything your old friend has ever done to you. Yet, God knows everything and still loves you and that other friend.

If God can forgive them for all their wrongdoings that they have done to Him, we can try to forgive the few wrongdoings that we know have been done to us. We should feel blessed we don't see and know everything God sees, or we would never forgive anyone.

Yet He still loves and forgives everyone if they ask for forgiveness. No one is too far gone to receive His grace and mercy. No one is beyond the grip of His hand to fall from His love. No one, not even your enemy, and not even you.

May you find time this Christmas season to show God you love Him and that you love others.

You may feel this is too large of a gift to give – forgiveness – but His grace and love is far, far greater. That is another thing that multiplies back: the more love and grace you give, the more you get in return.

May you come to God with your hands empty and your heart full and give Him all you have.

Each one must give as he has decided in his heart, not reluctantly or under compulsion, for God loves a cheerful giver. 2 Corinthians 9:7

But God shows his love for us in that while we were still sinners, Christ died for us. Romans 5:8

God,

I love you. Amen

Go Tell It on the Mountain
"When I was a seeker I sought both night and day"

When I was a kid, one of my favorite games to play in the neighborhood was hide-and-seek. We had various versions of this game, but the overlying theme was the same – one person counted while everyone else hid, and the counter had to seek and tag someone before they reached base. We used to play this game for hours.

I loved to be the hider. I used to try to find the best spot and sit and wait. There is something about sitting while holding your breath as the seeker is inches from finding you. That rush of not wanting to be found as your heartbeat increases knowing you could be tagged at any second if they just look down. Then the relief when they don't see you and you can finally take a deep breath when they walk away. Then once again you sit and wait until the coast is clear before darting out and running to the safety of base. Then you scream at the top of your lungs, "Safe!" or "Olly olly oxen free!"

Hide-and-seek is a classic game that kids love to play at all ages. Even adults sometimes fall to the temptation of playing the game with their kids or other adult friends.

But there were always those moments when my hiding spot wasn't good enough. Or my speed wasn't quick enough to get to base safely. Or I coughed during a crucial hiding moment and blew my cover. So I would become the seeker. I would count to a hundred with my eyes closed and then try to find my gang of friends. There may have been a dozen friends hiding, but I only had to find one. I didn't have to find everyone, just one.

If I found someone hiding they would take my title as seeker, and a new round would start. But if I didn't find anyone, I would continue to be the seeker until I could outsmart a hider.

Life is like a game of hide-and-seek. We are all hiding from something. We could be hiding from bullies that seem to never leave, hiding from our pasts with the baggage no one will buy at yard sales, hiding from chains that continue to haunt from bad decisions. We all hide. But more importantly, we are all seeking something too.

What are you looking for?

Because we are all seeking something, even if you don't think you are.

We all have a hole, a void, an emptiness we are hoping to fill. You may be trying to fill it with a relationship, whether friendly, family, or romantic. You may be hoping your career will fill the gap with promotions and working weekends. You may see alcohol or drugs as the filler that can seep into every crack and crevice. You may believe you don't have a chasm, but we all do.

You may not think you are seeking, and you may not be. You may be one of the many that have quit searching for the missing piece of the puzzle. But if you are honest with yourself, you can recall a season, a time period, a moment, or even a second where you were searching for something to fill you. You may have quit the expedition because it was useless. You may have failed so many times before looking for that elusive prize that you settled for something that didn't quite fit, but you would make due. You can duct tape your life so much that it seems like it is fixed, but eventually an air bubble will surface and it will start to unravel.

My garage door quit working recently. I messed with it for an hour trying to get it working again. Then I realized the person who previously fixed the garage door didn't fix it properly. They did something to fill the gap as a temporary fix. I watched videos on the internet for how to fix it, but none of the videos would work for my situation. So I searched some more. I never found a fix, but as I was searching I came up with an idea. I went to the hardware store a few times in my attempts, and I eventually found a fix. Would this fix be permanent or temporary?

Knowing my work skills, it might be temporary, and then I would have to figure something else out. But I searched for something to fill the gap. It may not have been the correct piece, but it would do.

How often in life do we settle for what will do instead of finding what we need?

When I was younger, I never considered "Go Tell It on a Mountain" a Christmas carol. We would sing it at church around Christmas, but I could also picture this song being sung all throughout the year. The only line that sounds like Christmas to me is "Our Jesus Christ is born" since Jesus' birth is highlighted at Christmas time.

But every time we sung it, it seemed to me that we should sing this song all year long. We should tell our family members in January that Jesus was born. We should tell our friends in February that Jesus was born. We should tell our co-workers, our neighbors, our waitress, our dental hygienist, our students every day of the year that Jesus Christ is born.

But we don't.

When was the last time you told someone about Jesus' birth?

I'm asking myself the same question and I cannot remember.

We sing the song on Sundays, but we don't tell the first person we see on Monday that Jesus Christ is born.

We don't tell because we assume they may already know, or if they wanted to know they would find a way to find out. We have some communities where a church is on almost every corner, so if someone wanted to find Jesus, they just have to open the door and come in.

Is that how you found Jesus?

Or did you find Him when someone led you to Him?

The line in this Christmas carol that stands out to me is,

"When I was a seeker I sought both night and day"

I love this line because I remember being a seeker. I remember wrestling with notions of faith and considering Jacob lucky to have proof of a God with his lasting limp. I wanted some proof. I wanted a limp like Jacob, or a fleece like Gideon, or a burning bush like Moses, or seeing a loved one rise from the dead like Lazarus. I wanted to know that God was real in a tangible way.

I was raised in church from birth, so it is not that I stopped believing in God for a period. I just stopped believing in the God everyone was telling me to believe in. I wanted to believe in the God *I* believed in. During this period in high school I clung to the Word. I knew the stories. I could recite the verses. But I was seeking Him. I trusted my family and my church, but I had to come to a point where I trusted God more than I trusted the people leading me to Him.

You may have heard stories of your great-great-great grandfather, but have never met him. He might have been a great man, but he died fifty years before you were born. You may hear brilliant, amazing, heartwarming stories of his accomplishments passed down through the generations. You may feel like you know everything about him, but the thing is, you still never met him. You never saw the moments that caused his legend to become bigger than life. You never heard him speak and dumbfound the city with his cunning skills. You never witnessed anything he did, so can you truly say you know him personally?

I think we are a society of so-called believers who have heard the stories of Jesus, have read the Bible, have seen miraculous moments that are undeniable, and we say we know him. Yet, we just know of him.

That period in high school showed me that I knew of Jesus, but I didn't truly personally know Him. So, I started seeking Him. I didn't lean on what other people said Jesus was, but I leaned into Him on who He said He was. There is a difference.

A few years ago, I tore my ACL. I had to have surgery and then walk on crutches for a month. I had to lean on a crutch to get by because my own leg wasn't strong enough. But eventually after rehab and gaining strength back into my leg, I was able to walk without a crutch.

People are using so many good things as a crutch to know God when God is saying, "I'm right here! Use the real thing! Don't use that crutch when you can have Me!"

So I ask again: what are you seeking?

You may think you have found God and He has filled that void. But you shouldn't rest on knowing God from three years ago. Like in a game of hide-and-seek, just because someone hid behind the tree three rounds ago doesn't mean they are going to hide there every time. Just because you found God three years ago, doesn't mean you can use that as a crutch for not seeking after Him continually.

Then when you find Him again, go and tell. Help people who are seeking to find him. Help people who don't even know they are wandering to meet what they are unknowingly searching for.

If you are one of the seekers looking for God night and day, don't lose hope. The search is worth it. It may be hard, but He wants you to find Him. If you are lost, ask someone for help. But ask someone who can help you find Him. Don't ask someone who will point you in the wrong direction. Sadly, there are many people out there who presume to know Him but don't. If something doesn't look right in your journey, just like if you are lost when you are driving, go and ask someone else for directions. Search parties don't have only one person looking, but many. Sometimes when we played hide-and-seek, if someone was having a hard time being the seeker, someone else would join his team and help. So for that round, there would be two seekers looking for all the hiders.

We are called to help one another. So if you are searching, get a partner, get a buddy, get a search party to help. Just don't fall into the temptation of using them as your crutch.

God is waiting, holding His breath, ready to be tagged.

And when you find Him, scream, "Olly olly oxen free!"

You will seek me and find me, when you seek me with all your heart. Jeremiah 29:13

Ask, and it will be given to you; seek, and you will find; knock, and it will be opened to you. Matthew 7:7

God,

Help me to find the real You. Amen

We Three Kings
"Glorious now behold Him arise"

Do you ever wake up in the morning and just want to stay in bed? The other morning I had this desire, but I had to go to work, so my wish of staying in bed a little longer was dashed. Then a few days later on my day off I awoke before my alarm would usually go off to get to work on time. And I just laughed at the irony. Well, maybe I didn't laugh at the time. I actually groaned and rolled my eyes at waking up when I could have slept longer.

But I can laugh about it now.

I know many people who are morning people. They think getting up early is glorious. They revel in getting up and moving before dawn, catching the early worm as some would say. I do admire these people. I have had fleeting moments of setting my alarm to wake up early to get into that habit of hitting the grind before the majority of the world.

Then when my alarm goes off early the next morning I hit the snooze button.

In those early mornings my ambition to take an early morning jog seems too ambitious. My plan to have a nice quiet time with God in the morning seems idiotic. My desire to arise early quickly loses its appeal.

I am not a morning person. But I have moments where I wish I was. Maybe one day I will change into one of those people, but until that change happens, I will hit the snooze button a few times each morning and groggily roll out of bed annoyed.

When I think of "We Three Kings" I cannot help but smile at the many times I have seen this song performed during children's plays in movies and television shows. Three kids are dressed in brightly colored robes with long gray beards tied on their faces and boxes and bottles in their hands. The Bible doesn't name these three kings, but tradition has given them the names of Balthasar, Melchior, and Gaspar (or Casper).

This beautiful hymn tells the story of the three kings traveling from distant lands bearing gifts for Jesus. The song changes through the stanzas from a Christmas song to an Easter song, but I have never heard the song sung at Easter. In the last stanza there is a beautiful reminder that Jesus' story isn't just about his birth. His birth was important, but it led to the triumphant story of his resurrection:

"Glorious now behold Him arise"

If there was not an Easter morning there would never be a Christmas morning. Christmas would just be December 25th with no great importance if Jesus hadn't risen from the dead.

But since He did arise, December 25th is very important.

I think we sometimes forget that Jesus' birth wasn't the beginning of the greatest story ever told. It was actually near the end.

God the Father was with Jesus the Son at the beginning of time. From the very beginning, God knew the important role Jesus was going to perform. From the very beginning, God the Father was with the Holy Spirit. From the very beginning, God knew the important role the Holy Spirit was going to perform after Jesus' resurrection.

If we look through the scriptures we can see glimpses of Jesus in the Old Testament as a foreshadow. From the story of the Garden of

Eden, to Melchizedek, to the life of Isaac, to the story of Jonah, to the fiery furnace, to the life of David, just to name a few. These are just a few of the foreshadows of Jesus.

Without the scriptures of the Old Testament, there would never have been anything to fulfill. But Jesus fulfilled all of the prophecies.

It is a glorious story that is worthy to be told and retold. But the greatest aspect of the story is when His friends and family witnessed the empty tomb. When they beheld the glory of a dead man's resting place with a mere folded sheet and angels.

Can you imagine?

We discussed the magnitude of the word 'behold' in reference to the birth of Jesus. But here we see the word in reference to His resurrected life.

Not to make light of His birth, because it was a monumental moment in time when God in flesh appeared to redeem the world, but I cannot fathom the feeling of His followers and foes when they heard or saw His once-dead body walking among the living. He arose not as a ghost or hallucination, but as a living man.

He arose with His wounds still on His hands and feet.

He arose to show death didn't have any claim on Him. He took on the sin of the world and died in all of our places so we wouldn't have to experience the separation from God, and then He arose.

It is one thing to experience a miracle today when a cancer suddenly vanishes, a wound suddenly heals, a supposed coincidence aligns perfectly, or a newborn's heartbeat is heard through the ultrasound. Miracles still happen, which should cause us to stop and behold the moment. But Jesus' resurrection is unlike anything I can imagine.

I can try to imagine the empty tomb where I had laid my friend a few days earlier. I can try to imagine the angels speaking of the reason for the emptiness. I can try to imagine the heart-stopping moment of confusion, the heart-racing moment of excitement, the speechless silence, the exuberant shouts of joy. I can try to imagine the glorious feeling of beholding that He arose from the dead.

But still, I cannot fully comprehend or imagine the screeching halt of going to the tomb to grieve to be told no grieving is needed.

It must have been glorious.

May we each come to Christ with whatever gifts we have and lay them at His feet. May we each come to Him with our empty hands and shortcomings, our pains and wounds, our burdens and failures. May we each come to Him and give Him everything we have, the good and the bad. May we come and behold Him.

But we cannot behold Him until we fully come to Him. Come to Him without any reservations. Come to Him as if running to an empty tomb. Come to Him with the excitement of witnessing the biggest star of all-time. Come to Him with thankfulness and gratitude. Come to Him with honor due to the King of Heaven. Come to Him with the sole purpose to behold Him.

But once again, we cannot behold Him until we fully come to Him.

I think it is time we come and behold Him because He rose.

And the glorious truth is He is still alive.

An even more glorious truth is He is waiting for us to come and behold Him. You are the reason He came to Earth in the first place. He came down to us so we can come now to Him.

Isn't that glorious?

On the glorious splendor of your majesty, and on your wondrous works, I will meditate. Psalm 145:5

Blessed be his glorious name forever; may the whole earth be filled with his glory! Amen and Amen! Psalm 72:19

God,

You are so glorious. Amen

References

Brooks, Phillips. "O Little Town of Bethlehem." Baptist Hymnal, Convention Press, 1956, p. 75.

Watts, Isaac. "Joy to the World! The Lord Is Come." Baptist Hymnal, Convention Press, 1956, p. 65.

Adam, Adolphe. "O Holy Night." Sudds, W.F., 1883, monographic.

Dix, William Chatterton. "What Child is This?" 1865.

Davis, Katherine K. "The Little Drummer Boy." 1941.

MacGimsey, Robert. "Sweet Little Jesus Boy." 1934.

Anonymous. "Away in a Manger." Baptist Hymnal, Convention Press, 1956, p. 77.

Traditional. "Angels We Have Heard on High." Baptist Hymnal, Convention Press, 1956, p. 64.

Montgomery, James. "Angels, from the Realms of Glory." Baptist Hymnal, Convention Press, 1956, p. 76.

Wesley, Charles. "Hark! The Herald Angels Sing." Baptist Hymnal, Convention Press, 1956, p. 81.

Regney, Noel. "Do You Hear What I Hear?" 1962.

Mohr, Joseph. "Silent Night, Holy Night." Baptist Hymnal, Convention Press, 1956, p. 72.

Van Dyke, Henry. "Joyful, Joyful, We Adore Thee." Baptist Hymnal, Convention Press, 1956, p. 44.

Wesley, Charles. "Hail, Thou Long-expected Jesus." Baptist Hymnal, Convention Press, 1956, p. 70.

Wade, John F. "O Come, All Ye Faithful." Baptist Hymnal, Convention Press, 1956, p. 66.

Traditional Latin Carol. "O Come, O Come, Emmanuel."

Medieval Latin Carol. "Good Christian Men, Rejoice." Baptist Hymnal, Convention Press, 1956, p. 74.

Old English Carol. "The First Noel the Angel Did Say." Baptist Hymnal, Convention Press, 1956, p. 63.

Sears, Edmund H. "It Came upon the Midnight Clear." Baptist Hymnal, Convention Press, 1956, p. 71.

Longfellow, Henry Wadsworth. "I Heard the Bells on Christmas Day." 1863.

English Traditional Carol. "God Rest You Merry, Gentlemen."

African-American Spiritual. "Go Tell It on the Mountain."

Hopkins, Jr. John Henry. "We Three Kings." 1857.

www.ingramcontent.com/pod-product-compliance
Lightning Source LLC
Chambersburg PA
CBHW071857020426

42331CB00010B/2560